Those Incomparable Bonanzas

by

Larry A. Ball

Published by
McCORMICK-ARMSTRONG CO., INCORPORATED
Publishing Division
1501 East Douglas Ave., Wichita, Kansas 67211

i

Walter H. Beech
(1891-1950)

"The Beechcraft Bonanza is a masterpiece of engineering; it's an airplane that constitutes a modern miracle of aeronautical design; and in our opinion, marks a new milestone in the progress of aviation."

— Walter H. Beech
August 1, 1946

Olive Ann Beech

This book is dedicated to

    — those who designed the Beechcraft Bonanza

    — those who manufacture and fly it

    — and especially to Mrs. Olive Ann Beech
        the first lady of aviation

ACKNOWLEDGEMENT

The writer is indebted to many for the assistance given over the years which made this book possible, but in particular to Herman Barnett, Jerry Gordon, Alex Odevseff, Noel Naidenoff, and Robert T. Smith.

Larry A. Ball

Contents

Preface

I believe this book will be the most complete history ever recorded of the Beechcraft Bonanza. That has certainly been my intention, and probably no other individual will have been privileged with the information and have access to the wealth of data that has been a part of my life for the past fifteen years.

Actually, my association with the Bonanza goes back farther than that. I can still remember the first Bonanza to land at my home town airport in Ponca City, Oklahoma, in 1947. And I certainly will never forget the first time I ever sat in one as a 15-year-old line boy and taxied it away from the gas pump to a tie-down. What an entirely different airplane from the J-3 Cubs on our field!

The next encounter was as a senior in high school, when Bill Odom, fresh from his record-breaking non-stop flight, was scheduled to land for a brief stop during a tour of Oklahoma towns. Four or five of us skipped school that day to be on hand to greet him, not knowing his short stay would be devoted to a talk at our high school. My next recollection is a hitchhike in the rear seat of a Bonanza from Birmingham, Alabama, to Memphis, Tennessee, in the summer of 1951.

Then the moment. It was June 29, 1953, and I was in Arkansas City, Kansas. The fixed base operator asked me to take a customer's Bonanza back to Ponca City for a 100-hour inspection. I had a Commercial License and a Flight Instructor Rating, but not one minute behind the wheel of this Queen of the single engine fleet. Too eager and too proud to tell him I had never flown a Bonanza, I said I would, then waited patiently for him to leave for lunch before firing up. Rather, it was not so much a case of firing up, but quietly sitting in the cabin and reading the Owner's Manual on how to take-off, climb, and cruise the Bonanza, then land it. This was the first airplane I had ever flown that had an Owner's Manual, and it was understandably a welcome addition to the loose equipment.

My log book records a 15-minute flight from Arkansas City to Ponca City that day in Bonanza N3884N. As I recall, I left the landing gear down to be on the safe side, that would account for it taking 15 minutes to go only 28 miles. Still, it was a far cry from the prewar, rag wing Luscombe I had left in Arkansas City.

It was not my fortune to sit in a Bonanza again until 1957, when I joined Beech Aircraft Corporation, became a member of the Beechcraft Employees Flying Club, and was honored to fly one of the "R" series Bonanzas, a rebuilt straight 35. Then later, I administered the service tests of the first fuel injected J35 Bonanzas for the company, and my logged Bonanza time grew rapidly.

The idea for this book came much later. It was during 1964 that I realized someone, sooner or later, must write a complete and accurate history of the airplane that had become the standard of the industry. Few of the people originally associated with the Bonanza were still at Beech. However, by now, I knew most of them, or at least where they could be located, and I would be able to pick up with my own experience where theirs left off. Thus I became convinced the task was mine.

This book was begun in 1965, and it has been a labor of love from the very start. Encouragement has come from many sources, but most particularly from my wife Linda and from Dr. B. J. McClanahan, Founder and first President of the American Bonanza Society.

It is my hope this book will not only provide interesting reading for the Bonanza enthusiast and owner, but be of value to anyone considering ownership of any model of the Beechcraft Bonanzas. Part I deals with the design in general, Part II with the specifics of each model of this long and ageless line of "the finest single engine airplane ever built!"

Larry A. Ball
October, 1971

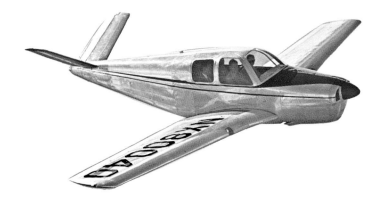

The Story Behind the Name

In 1946 Walter Beech announced his all new, revolutionary single engine entry in the postwar market. It was to be called the "Bonanza". In announcing the company's choice of this name, Beech explained, "Airplanes have been named after stars, galaxies, constellations, animals, fish, birds, and natural phenomena such as hurricanes, lightning, and thunderbolts. For our new Model 35, Beech Aircraft has sought to find a name that would be descriptive of the extra value offered in the way of economy, performance, and pleasure to the owner. We examined the word 'Bonanza' which in English has the common meaning of a rich source of profit or gain, or an unusual value.

"We found that it has the same general meaning in other languages and also has an additional meaning of fair weather in certain foreign languages. This seemed to be consistent with the fact that the Beechcraft Bonanza has a built-in tail wind. To a pilot, fair weather obviously implies a tail wind and the Bonanza has it as standard equipment.

"Literal translations are as follows:
      Spanish — Bonanza. Translation: Prosperity, success, fair weather.
      Portuguese — Bonanca. Translation: Prosperity, success, calm, fair weather.
      French — Bonace. Translation: Calm, smooth sea, tranquility.
      Italian — Bonaccia. Translation: Prosperity, welfare, calm, tranquility.

"Summing up all the meanings of 'Bonanza' in English and in other languages, we feel that 'Bonanza' is a fit name for our new airplane. We have designed it for the prosperity, success and pleasure of its owners and we are certain that it will fulfill those requirements."

One of the
100 "Best Designed" Products

In 1958 Mr. Jay Doblin, Director of the Institute of Design of the Illinois Institute of Technology, undertook the ambitious project of determining the 100 best-designed, mass-produced products of modern times. He selected 100 of the world's leading designers, architects, and design teachers and asked that they in turn select their top ten choices.

The Beechcraft Bonanza was included in this list which was later published in the April, 1959 issue of Fortune Magazine. The only other aircraft included in the 100 best designed list was another world famous airplane, the Douglas DC-3.

Bonanza Firsts

The Bonanza was described as the first all new postwar design to enter the commercial market. Here is the impressive list of aviation "firsts" for its class owned by this revolutionary design.

First — with electrically retractable tricycle landing gear completely enclosed inside the wing and nose.

First — to carry four people at a cruising speed of 175 MPH.

First — to carry a full payload, fully equipped, for its full range.

First — to be fully equipped for day, night, and instrument flight as standard equipment.

First — with an automatically retracting entrance and exit step.

First — with the distinctive, aerodynamically cleaner V-tail.

First — with adjustable cowl flaps.

First — to include as standard equipment a two-way, three-band direction-finding radio.

First — to achieve a significantly lower level in interior quietness.

First — to provide as standard a luxury of appointments comparable to the most expensive automobile.

First — to provide landing lights streamlined into the leading edge of the wing to reduce drag.

First — to completely enclose the directional loop antenna in the tail for reduced drag.

First — to offer a four-position control wheel for greater flying ease.

First — to use flush riveting, reducing drag to a minimum.

First — to provide baggage accessibility comparable with an automobile.

The continued success of the Bonanza today is simple proof that Beech was a quarter of a century ahead of other general aviation manufacturers when he first introduced the Bonanza.

Max Karant, Vice President of the Aircraft Owners and Pilots Association, after first flight in the Beechcraft Bonanza. 1946.

"The average personal planes today are not nearly what they should be, in view of what our aeronautical engineers actually know. They are uncomfortable, noisy, harder-to-fly than they should be . . . but things are looking up. I've already flown a contemporary personal plane that cruises at more than 170 mph and lands at 46." A quote from Max Karant's speech to the National Aviation Clinic at Oklahoma City in 1946. Karant was then editor of Flying Magazine.

Photo of first flight — December 22, 1945. Vern L. Carstens, then Beech Aircraft's chief test pilot (now retired), is at the controls.

How It Began

1944. The allied invasion of France. The conquest of the Japanese in the Marianas. If the American public was thinking of airplanes at all they were contemplating the Flying Fortresses and Liberators bombing Germany in 2000 airplane waves, or the massive air battles in the Pacific where Navy Hellcats and Corsairs were downing hundreds of Japanese fighters. America's light plane manufacturers were busy — but busy turning out military versions of their prewar offerings or serving as subcontractors for larger airframe manufacturers, or doing both. Waco was building gliders, Stinson the L-5 Sentinel liaison airplane — at Lock Haven Piper was producing the L-4 Grasshopper, training gliders, and aerial ambulances.

In Wichita, Kansas, Cessna concentrated its efforts on production of the military version of the prewar twin engine Cessna T-50. In military garb the T-50 was known as the Army Air Force's AT-17 and UC-78, the Navy's JRC-1. The "Bobcat" was being used for twin engine pilot training and personnel transportation. Culver was active, building small radio controlled target planes for both services. At Boeing the old Stearman plant was turning out record numbers of "Kaydet" open cockpit biplane trainers. Giant B-29 bombers were rolling out of Boeing's big Plant II. Even Swallow Aircraft was active. They operated a school which provided trained personnel for the other factories.

Across town at Beech the twin engine Model 18 was being produced in a variety of configurations to meet the training and transport needs of both services. In a way the Bonanza owes a lot to the Model 18. It was because Beech had the versatile 18 proven and in production when war broke out that they were an early selection to provide the military with twin engine pilot, bombardier, and navigator trainers. Compared to what other general aviation manufacturers were building at the time the all metal, high performance Twin Beech represented quite a few steps in aeronautical progress. The manufacturing capability quickly developed by the company in order for them to deliver military versions of the 18 in quantity also made them a logical choice for such subcontracts as the production of wings for the Douglas A26 Invader attack bomber.

All of this activity added up to rapidly advancing manufacturing capability and improved technology. A completely new airplane had been designed and produced — the Beechcraft AT-10. Over 1700 were manufactured and placed in service as twin engine pilot trainers. Beech even designed and flew their own combat airplane, the XA-38 "Grizzly". Although the war would end before the Grizzly would see production it was an impressive achievement. With a nose mounted 75 mm cannon it was an ideal anti-tank weapon — yet it was as fast as the fighter planes of that time.

1

Twin Beech production line at height of war effort.

A complete set of Invader wings rolled off every hour.

THE AT-10 "WICHITA" (Beech Model 26)

Foreseeing a shortage of aluminum, Beech elected to design the Model 26 to be fabricated mostly of wood. The AT-10 was the first all-wood type to be accepted as an advanced trainer by the U. S. Army. It was made entirely of wood with the exception of the engine nacelles and cowling, pilot's compartment, landing gear and engine support structure, and essential fittings and connections. No double-curvature sections were used and no hot-molding processes were necessary in the forming of the various wooden parts. Because of this it was possible for furniture manufacturers and similar wood working organizations to undertake the building of major sub-assemblies. Subcontractors accounted for 85 percent of the parts.

The Beechcraft X-38 Grizzly attack bomber. The nose mounted 75-mm. cannon was intended for enemy tanks.

The Grizzly had two remotely controlled turrets, each with a pair of 50 calibre machine guns. The bottom turret is clearly visible here. Notice also the C-45 in the background with British Roundel.

3

This, then was the atmosphere at the Beech factory during 1944. They were busy with the war effort, and their particular share of the task was giving them a "leg up" on what would be their postwar competitors. It was considered almost unpatriotic to be thinking ahead to the postwar years — but imagination can be difficult to quell. What would they build after the war was over? Certainly the Twin Beech. It was ideally suited to continue its earlier role as twin engine executive transportation, and there would not likely be anything on the market to challenge it for years to come. But the Model 17 Staggerwing was a question mark. Beech was currently producing it for the military (it was a great conserver of aluminum) but the war had accelerated developments in the industry and the biplane was definitely on its way out. In addition, the higher labor costs generated by the war would make the mostly handmade Model 17 a very expensive airplane to build. Then there was the continuing trend to all metal construction in light planes which Luscombe had started as early as 1934 with a metal fuselage. It was obvious an all new design was called for if Beech was to enjoy a substantial share of the single engine market. So the task wouldn't interfere with the war effort, five Beech engineers began working nights and weekends, doing preliminary design engineering on a completely new single engine Beechcraft.

Ted Wells, then Beech Vice President of Engineering, put Ralph Harmon in charge of the project. Harmon had been after Wells for some time to begin such a program, now he had his chance! All work was to be done on a voluntary, overtime basis. Harmon was the overall project engineer and gave himself the additional responsibility of interior and landing gear design.

The Bonanza predecessor, the famous Beechcraft Model 17 Staggerwing.

Working with him were Jerry Gordon, Alex Odevseff, Noel Naidenoff, and Wilson Erhart. Gordon was Beech's Chief of Aerodynamics and was responsible for the shape of the wings and all surfaces. Erhart then designed the wing structure. Alex Odevseff tackled the fuselage design while Noel Naidenoff developed the fuel system and engine support structure.

What kind of airplane to build? What kind of airplanes could the competition be expected to build? Some were already expressing themselves. Globe Aircraft Corporation in Fort Worth was advertising a postwar model of its small low wing monoplane known as the "Swift". Two place, all metal, and with retractable conventional landing gear, the Swift was certificated in 1942 but not produced. They would presumably be ready to go after the cessation of hostilities. Taylorcraft and Luscombe were talking up prewar models, and Bellanca was conducting a postwar "aircraft quiz" in an effort to determine what the market *really* wanted.

Piper could be counted on to continue with production of the popular J-3 Cub and J-5 Cruiser. Wichita barber shop talk had it that Cessna would be coming out with a new two place training and personal aircraft. Aeronca would surely start up their "Chief" and "Defender" series. They were also flying a new low wing airplane similar to the Culver Cadet which they called the "Arrow". And there were new companies entering the market. One with the unlikely name of "Hockaday" was touting its entry called the "Comet".

Surplus airplanes would also be on the market. Already Aeroncas, Taylorcrafts, Stinsons, Interstates, and Ryans were showing up as surplus to defense

The Piper Cub J-3 Special.

TAYLORCRAFT   AERONCA CHAMPION

CESSNA 140   AERONCA ARROW

A variety of two place airplanes flooded the market after World War II ended. Most were simply reworked prewar offerings. The all new Cessna 140 was the only successful exception — other new designs either never left the drawing board or faltered shortly after production began.

needs. OPA (Office of Price Administration) prices ranged from $1788 for a nearly new Aeronca L-3B to $6736 for a Stinson Reliant.

Of course, this was the period when it was popular to talk about postwar aviation in terms of an airplane in every garage, or at least every back yard. After all, the war effort had resulted in the training of thousands of pilots, and even more important, every GI would have been exposed to aviation in one way or another. The GI Bill that Congress had recently passed would provide flight training for all veterans who wanted it. Sunday supplements carried rosy predictions of an "everyman's airplane". These stories made exciting reading for the public, and for even some people in the industry, but they were obviously pipe dreams to experienced airplane manufacturers. Flying had been, and would continue to be, a relatively expensive pastime. There was even frequent talk of the postwar role for rotary wing aircraft — that helicopters and autogyros would be taking over the bulk of the short haul requirements of air transportation. And many, it seems, correlated peace with going fishing — their postwar airplane must be an amphibian, or at the very least capable of operation on floats. The pusher versus tractor argument began anew and at least one manufacturer, Waco, was considering a pusher they called the "Aristocrat". Also revived were discussions of flying autos and roadable airplanes.

It is interesting to note here that J. Carlton Ward, then President of Fairchild Engine and Airplane Corporation, had this to say about the postwar dream plane during the latter part of 1944. "The postwar plane, which recent consumer surveys indicate the public thinks should cost about $1500 to $2500 would, under present conditions, cost approximately $13,500.* Standard equipment for such a ship, which would carry four or five passengers and their baggage in comfort equal to that of the automobile, but with a 500-mile range and at a speed of 150 MPH, would alone cost $12,150. Extras called for by the surveys, in the form of radio, instrumentation, lights, soundproofing and ventilation, would add another $1386." Ward also took issue with the theory that wartime mass production experience had evolved more efficient and cheaper methods of turning out airplane parts. Asserting that since at maximum, the industry had turned out only 10,000 airplanes a month, "it will therefore be seen that there is no mass production of airplanes comparable to that of the automobile industry".

There were also voices pointing out that even if the ideal airplane could be mass produced and sold for $2000, the market just wasn't there to support real volume production — the airplane would not, in the foreseeable future, become the necessity the automobile had become, even with a $2000 price

*Although the original Bonanzas sold for $7975, after five years of production experience the price had reached Ward's $13,000.

An admirable attempt made by Piper to develop an airplane to sell for $1000. Known as the Piper "Skycycle", the single place airplane was not produced because the cost of materials alone nearly equalled the hoped for selling price.

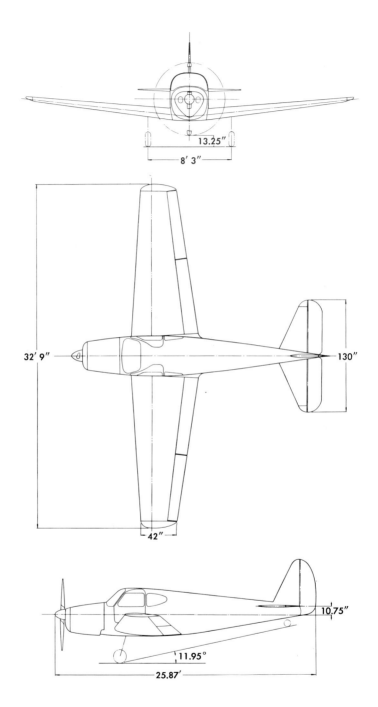

13.25"

8' 3"

32' 9"

130"

42"

10.75"

11.95°

25.87'

Beech Aircraft's first design study for a postwar airplane, the Model 33.
A limited four place airplane, this concept was abandoned and the Model
35 conceived. The Model 33 designation was picked up fifteen years later
and applied to the Debonair.

Full scale, wooden mockup of Model 33 fuselage and tail.

tag. Naturally, this kind of unimaginative talk was largely ignored by the press — in favor of the latest artist's conception of a roadable dream plane, stored in the family garage.

In the midst of all this fanciful speculation the Beech team of designers had to come up with a new airplane — one based on the real world of hard aeronautical and economic facts. In their favor was the production experience of all metal airplanes gained on the Model 18. Also in their favor was the fact they were about the only general aviation manufacturer with this knowledge. True, there were other aircraft manufacturers, such as Republic and North American, with the same design and manufacturing know-how, but they had no experience in the general aviation market.

The Beech team ruled out the small, two-place type very early in their study. Such a plane would conceivably fall in the price range the public wanted, but have little utility and be relegated for the most part to training functions. The training plane market slot would be quickly crowded with Aeroncas, Pipers, Cessnas, and Taylorcrafts.

Walter Beech had built his reputation by manufacturing swift, dependable airplanes with good comfort, range, and payload — this was still the challenge to be met. The design team's initial efforts were aimed at development of a limited four place ship with modest power — in reality, a three place airplane. The production cost of such an airplane would allow for very competitive pricing. It wasn't long before this concept was also ruled out. Price alone wouldn't accomplish the company's objective. Everyone became convinced the goal must be a full-size, four-place airplane.

They felt the new Beechcraft should have adequate baggage space for four people and carry enough fuel for flights of a practical length. It should be equipped with instruments and night flying equipment to enable flight in any reasonable weather — and finally, it should be fast enough to match or exceed the speeds of current commercial airliners. In other words a modern airplane, and a true Staggerwing replacement.

9

The airplane would, of course, be all metal. It was also decided it should have maximum eye appeal. To accomplish this an automobile stylist, Wayne Porter, was brought into the program. A cost survey indicated the airplane would have to sell for a price somewhere between $6000 and $7000. (The first Bonanzas actually sold for $7975. As a comparison, the few postwar G17S Staggerwings produced sold for $29,000.) The target price was to include all normally used equipment as standard to the airplane. At this point layouts of a design were made incorporating these objectives. To arrive at a cabin size considered adequate and comfortable for four people a Mercury automobile was used to establish interior dimensions.

The choice of a power plant was critical to the design. It became apparent early that a radial engine was not practical for the airplane being considered. Forward vision would be unsatisfactory. It was also doubtful a propeller could be used that would be large enough to provide best performance yet maintain sufficient ground clearance. A high thrust line and a low cowl were a necessity. This left the engine choice between a flat or an inverted type. It also had to be air cooled.

There were no power plants in existence that completely met the design needs. Lycoming and Continental were contacted to see if they would be interested in supplying engines to meet the specific requirements of the program. A market analysis had indicated demand would justify development of an engine for this general application.

All landing gear configurations were considered for the new airplane. Fixed conventional, fixed tricycle, retractable conventional, and retractable tricycle. There were good arguments for each configuration. Properly designed aerodynamically, a fixed tricycle gear would provide minimum drag and be the most reliable for a pilot with limited experience. A fixed conventional gear would be the least expensive to produce. However, since performance as well as utility ranked high on the list of design objectives, these arguments were not enough. At a time when most other general aviation manufacturers would have been happy just to retract their gear — Beech elected to go with the most sophisticated arrangement, the retractable tricycle gear, and then completely enclose it in the wing and nose section.

With this selection of landing gear the engine choice was further restricted. It appeared nearly impossible to use an inverted engine and still have room to retract the nose wheel. A "flat" engine would be required. Lycoming and Continental were each asked to make a proposal. They were asked to limit propeller revolutions to 2050 RPMs or less in order to maintain a high degree of propeller efficiency. To obtain the desired performance the design team specified 150 horsepower as the minimum acceptable.

Lycoming proposed a small four cylinder engine of 290 cubic inches displacement which they would turn at 3000 RPM. It would have a reduction drive to lower the propeller speed to a maximum of 1925 RPM. Continental Motors suggested a six cylinder engine of 475 cubic inches with a direct drive turning the propeller at 2050 RPM. Each company agreed to give their

10

Lycoming's entry for the Bonanza. The first Bonanza to fly used this power-plant. (1945)

The first Bonanza production engine, the Continental E-165-4. (1945)

engine a maximum continuous rating of 165 horsepower. Both engines looked good, so it was decided to give both proposals a try. This was one of the first attempts by an airframe manufacturer designing a small plane to insist on an engine design embodying characteristics to give the airplane maximum performance.

Beech decided to go the expense of complete wind tunnel testing in an effort to develop the most efficient airframe possible. At this time few small airplanes had ever had the benefit of a wind tunnel test program. Jerry Gordon headed this effort. The wind tunnel model was made as large as practical to eliminate scale effects. One-fifth scale, it had a wing span of 6½ feet. A ten horsepower high speed electric motor and scale propeller were installed so it would more nearly simulate an airplane in flight. This enabled Gordon to determine the effects of power on stability and control. Performance estimates made prior to the wind tunnel work indicated a sea level high speed of 160 MPH would be possible. Early wind tunnel efforts revealed 165 MPH might be reached, so the project looked even more promising.

Two different wing designs were tested in the tunnel: The NACA 23000 series airfoil previously used on the Model 18 Twin Beech and the XA-38 attack bomber, and a new laminar flow wing. The North American P-51 and other fighter aircraft had popularized laminar flow, and it was unquestionably a benefit in drag reduction in the higher speed ranges. There was even rumor that North American would be coming out with an all-metal, four-place family airplane flying on a laminar flow wing.

Wind tunnel results gave the old Beech standby, the 23000 series airfoil, the edge. In the speed ranges the airplane would be flying the difference in drag was scarcely measurable, and the 23000 wing displayed better flight characteristics. (However, since so much was riding on this development program it was later decided to go ahead and test both wings in actual flight.)

Another area of possible drag reduction showed more promise — the tail design. During 1943 Beech had investigated a V-tail as a part of a design study for a high speed airplane. Compressibility (velocities approaching the speed of sound) was being observed for the first time in the higher speed military aircraft. It appeared a V-tail, sitting high on the fuselage of a low wing airplane, would be out of the turbulent wake caused by the breakdown of airflow over the wing at critical speeds. Beech had conducted wind tunnel tests, and later flew a V-tail on an experimental AT-10. While compressibility would hardly be a problem in the speed range under consideration, the V-tail did have other benefits that might make it desirable for the new airplane.

The AT-10 application achieved a reduction in total tail area with an attendant reduction in drag. The reduced surface-to-fuselage intersections also contributed to lower drag. Cruise speed was higher by 3 MPH when compared to the conventional tailed AT-10s. No significant weight saving occurred with this particular installation, but both Harmon and Gordon felt a savings would be possible if the V-tail were part of the initial airplane design. Considering the long moment arm, any savings would be worthwhile from the

Wind tunnel tests of V-Tail. This particular testing was being done for the AT-10 application.

13

standpoint of weight and balance. They became the leading boosters for application of this tail to the new Beechcraft.

In addition to reduced weight and drag, it also offered the possibility of lower manufacturing costs through fewer parts, and there would be fewer parts for dealers to stock. Still another factor in favor of the V-tail was the reduced risk from ground damage from rocks thrown back by the wheels.

Flight tests in the AT-10 had also revealed the V-tail had superior spin recovery characteristics to that of many conventional tails. On some airplanes the horizontal stabilizer, in the stalled condition, tends to blanket out the airflow past the rudder and part of the vertical fin, causing reduced rudder effectiveness. The V-tailed AT-10 spin recovery had been superior to the standard configuration.

In the AT-10 application a dihedral of 40 degrees had been used to give satisfactory engine-out control. Gordon felt a 30 degree dihedral would be a good compromise between the requirements of directional and longitudinal stability for a single engine airplane. This angle then was selected for use in the wind tunnel. Again, the wind tunnel model was tested with both a V-tail and conventional surfaces, and the tests revealed the "V" to be equal to the conventional tail in controllability, but as predicted, a lower drag producing configuration.

While the wind tunnel work was progressing other members of the design team were busy with hardware. Ralph Harmon was having difficulty finding good, lightweight instruments and particularly instruments with any style. By working hard with the various instrument manufacturers he and Wayne Porter, in the end, achieved an instrument panel design considerably ahead of its time. Noel "Roosh" Naidenoff was trying to keep the weight of the engine accessories down by combining the oil tank and oil cooler. He also conserved space in the cabin by combining the fuel selector and wobble pump. Wilson Erhart busied himself with wing structural details, and, like the rest, was attempting to keep weight down and performance up. Walter Beech had insisted the airplane be able to carry a full complement of what was ordinarily considered to be options, and four people, and baggage!

A market analysis had indicated Beech could expect to sell from two to four thousand of this type of airplane a year so a relatively high level of production had to be kept in mind. It was planned to make maximum use of Beech's "Erco" automatic riveting machines. These machines could drive flush rivets as easily as round, or "brazier" head rivets. Hand driven flush rivets, on the other hand, were quite expensive. The wing was designed so it could be fabricated and assembled as four sub-assemblies and then mated. The wing leading edge section, the main spar and the intermediate or "box" section were designed to be joined together with a piano hinge. The main object of the piano hinge was to avoid riveting in difficult and relatively inaccessible areas but it had the additional advantage of allowing the leading edge of the wing to be removed to facilitate repair in the field.

This is the only known photograph of the Bonanza wind tunnel model. It was 1/5 scale giving it a wing span of 6½ feet.

Alex Odevseff carried the same philosophy into the fuselage design. Detail assemblies going together to form major subassemblies, then ultimately mating of the entire fuselage. He succeeded in developing a breakout of assemblies which would allow the cabin section, tail section, and "keel" or engine compartment to be fabricated and assembled separately, then joined in a fuselage mating jig.

Beech wasn't the only manufacturer attempting to incorporate war learned production lessons into a new design. Out on Long Island, New York, Republic Aviation was busy developing a four-place, all-metal amphibian to sell for under $4000. This would only be possible if the hopes of their President, Alfred Marchev, were realized. He was pressuring his engineers to reduce the number of airframe parts from 1800 to just a few hundred, the man-hours from 2500 to under 200. And the just announced North American Navion could also be expected to utilize the latest manufacturing techniques.

But many labor and material saving ideas compromised the vital area of performance. Heavy beaded skins, for example, weigh more and increase aerodynamic drag. The Beech team was determined their entry would provide the most performance per horsepower. Walter wanted his new postwar design to be in a class by itself in all respects, but particularly in efficiency. An all-out effort was therefore exerted to produce the most aerodynamically clean external configuration possible.

15

An early Bonanza cowl styling effort. Very close to the final selection.

The V-tail was an important contribution in this area but work didn't stop there. A maximum amount of flush riveting of exterior skins was called for, as well as flush windshield joints, not only fully retractable but completely enclosed landing gear, internal flap tracks, and all control surfaces internally hinged. In addition the entrance step would have to retract, and the power plant section would use adjustable cowl flaps rather than a fixed, drag producing cooling gill. Flap gap doors were added to the wings to further reduce drag.

Mockup of Bonanza with laminar flow wing, 1945.

Jerry Gordon estimated the cowl flaps were worth 6 MPH, the retractable step 3 MPH, the smooth flush windshield design another 3 MPH, the "V" or butterfly tail as they now chose to call it, 5 MPH, flush riveting 3 MPH, internally balanced and hinged control surfaces 3 MPH, flap gap doors 4 MPH. He also estimated that completely enclosing the landing gear after retraction added another 5 MPH. This airplane would have the lowest coefficient of drag in its class!

A great deal of care was taken to insure the new design would incorporate features providing maximum safety for occupants. Studies made by the Cornell University Safety Research Group and other leading authorities were used, as well as Beech Aircraft's own investigations. To begin with, the airplane would be a low wing design which afforded good protection for the passengers in the event of a forced landing. Over 80 percent of the airplane's weight would be below or ahead of the passenger compartment. It would have a long nose section to provide gradual impact deceleration. The heavy underneath keel section would extend from the nose to just aft of the trailing edge of the wing and provide additional protection from the ground in a gear-up landing.

The cabin was designed as a strong, crash resistant compartment. To provide a turnover structure deep box sections were run up each side of the windshield to the cabin top. They then branched out with one branch crossing over and above the windshield and the other running aft above the window line and joining similar box sections rising between the front and rear windows. There was still another box section aft of the rear windows. These sections contained many complicated shapes and created a difficult, and therefore expensive tooling problem. They were considered necessary, however, to meet the company's goal of high crash survivability.

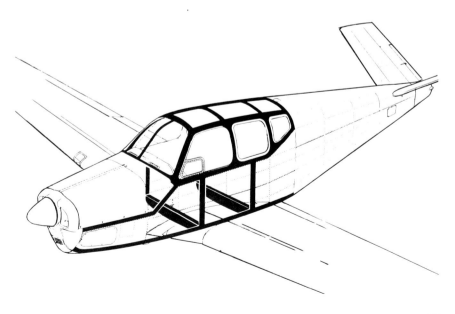

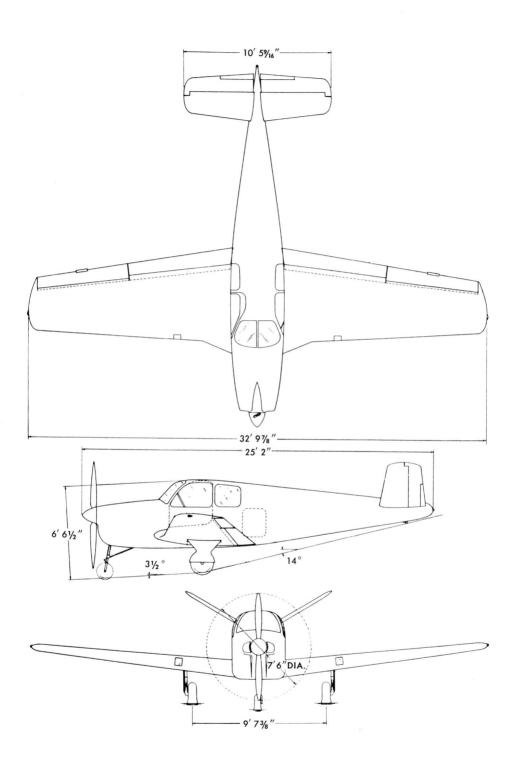

10' 5⁹⁄₁₆"

32' 9⁷⁄₈"

25' 2"

6' 6½"

3½°

14°

7' 6" DIA.

9' 7³⁄₈"

18

Preproduction unit number 5 undergoing fatigue test.

As a part of their overall safety program the designers included emergency escape exits should the main door become jammed in a crash. The rear windows were made not only large but openable and provided with quick release pins. By pulling the pins the windows would release at the bottom and open completely as emergency exits. This would be one airplane that could be evacuated in seconds!

As detail engineering became available parts were made to build five pre-production prototypes. Before the first airplane would fly, however, a pro-gram of unprecedented fatigue testing would be conducted in the laboratory. Two of the airplanes were subjected to the equivalent of 20,000 hours of flying in order to make certain that fatigue failures would not occur. This work was in addition to and supplemental to the normal static tests required by the then CAA. Laboratory simulated landings were conducted using a com-plete wing and landing gear assembly for 100,000 landings.

In the area of static tests each major component was designed, built, and tested to destruction. If the structure showed evidence of carrying less than the maximum design load, the test was stopped and the structure reinforced to obtain the desired strength.

Control surfaces were exposed to the high frequency vibrations that could be generated by the engine or by surface flutter. These tests resulted in localized reinforcing to insure long service life. It is doubtful any other single engine, general aviation airplane ever went through such an extensive program of laboratory testing — all this before the design had even left the ground!

Wing vibration fatigue test, 1945.

After many months of wind tunnel, fatigue, and static tests the moment arrived for flight tests to begin. The first airplane to fly would use the laminar flow wing and the new Lycoming, the GO-290, rated at 165 HP. Vern Carstens, Beech's veteran chief test pilot, who had also first flown the 30,000-pound, pursuit-speed XA-38 Grizzly, was the natural choice for that first flight. After several days of taxi runs on Beech's mile long airstrip, on December 22, 1945, just a little more than four months from V-J Day, Carstens headed the airplane that was to become known as the "Bonanza" into the wind and added throttle. The Bonanza was off on its maiden flight.

Although a great deal of work remained between that flight and the time when production airplanes would roll down the assembly line, when Carstens set the Bonanza down, 40 minutes later, Walter Beech had the answer to his question, "were our plans and ambitions for this airplane justified?" Carstens' answer was, "It's the best airplane we've built yet!"

High speed cruise was 175 MPH, or 10 MPH over wind tunnel calculations. This first airplane was tested about 50 hours. The second airplane to fly used the NACA 23000 series wing and the Continental engine, which also developed 165 HP. Speed tests revealed the airplanes to be nearly identical. Both were capable of a cruise speed of 175 MPH. The wind tunnel tests, however, were proven out. The 23000 wing proved to be a better all-around wing and so became the final selection for production.

The engine choice was more difficult to make. The Continental was a few pounds lighter, but it occupied more space and had a more complicated exhaust manifold. The Lycoming was four cylinder, and there had been some

Bonanza laminar flow wing in flight, 1946. Photo plane appears to be a Fairchild PT-19.

concern it would be rougher than the six cylinder Continental but in actual trials it was just as smooth. Selection of the Continental was finally made due to earlier delivery.

The right propeller was vital to the program not only for performance but cabin sound level. A propeller had to be designed to give maximum performance at the relatively low RPMs selected for optimum cabin sound level and good propeller efficiency. Here Beech was one up on every other general aviation manufacturer — for Beechcraft had pioneered in the development of controllable propellers for light planes. Hundreds of Beechcraft propellers were manufactured during the war to increase the performance of many of the armed services aircraft. Hundreds more were already being produced for postwar personal and business aircraft owners who wanted quicker take-off, better climb, faster cruising, and more economy. With all this experience behind them, Beech engineering eagerly began designing their own propeller for the Bonanza.

The experimental flight test program was exhaustive, and, as might be expected changes were made. The stall characteristics were good but made better by the installation of small stall strips located about one-third of the way out on the leading edge of the wing. This allowed the Bonanza to stall under full power and yet settle with the wings level.

It was originally hoped that 45 degrees of maximum flap deflection could be used to obtain the lowest possible landing speed, however with this much flap the Bonanza would not meet the CAA's minimum trim requirements.

The requirement stated that it must be possible to level out to landing attitude with the trim tab alone in the event of an elevator control cable failure. Compliance with this requirement limited the maximum flap deflection to 20 degrees. This resulted in an increase in flap down stalling speed from 46 MPH to 55 MPH.

Even with this limitation on the flaps an increase in elevator chord of about two inches was found desirable and incorporated. Engine cooling initially was a problem but was soon brought under control through the addition of internal baffles and the shielding of the exhaust mufflers.

Then an accident occurred with one of the test airplanes. During a series of dive tests in which the pilot was attempting to establish VD (highest dive velocity) flutter was encountered in the tail which caused the balance weights to be thrown from the surfaces. The surfaces separated from the fuselage and the test airplane, along with its pilot, were lost. The observer on board parachuted to safety, reported what had happened, and engineering changes were begun immediately.

While the accident didn't slow down the Bonanza development program appreciably, it was aviation news, and received wide publicity and speculation. Few private aircraft had ever received so much advance word-of-mouth build-up as the Bonanza, and now, as a result of the accident, the "anti" rumors would be equally strong. Compared with some other general aviation manufacturers, Beech was already late in hitting the market. There had previously been talk the airplane would never leave the drawing boards, now the accident would create new speculation.

He had been first to the marketplace with the Model 18. Only two months after Japan had surrendered, the first civilian 18 had rolled from the assembly line, but he was unquestionably running late with his single engine entry. North American would soon begin to deliver at least a few Navions. This airplane would be directly competitive with the Bonanza and was priced at $6100. Republic was even delivering the widely acclaimed SeaBee, and at a price of $4495. Apparently Marchev had achieved his goal and was building the four-place amphibian with greatly reduced manhours. And the smaller planes were out. Piper was delivering Cubs as fast as they could build them; Marshall Field in Chicago was displaying Ercoupes and had reportedly sold 40 in the first month; Cessna was delivering their new two-place 140.

But Walter Beech would not be hurried into taking short cuts. If an orderly and thorough program required time, then so be it. In fact, even though the experimental flight test program had been exhaustive, he called for an extensive service test program as soon as there were airplanes available. Three Bonanzas were used. Flying a 170-mile circuit course and using ten airport facilities of all types, service test pilots accumulated 500 to 600 hours on each Bonanza. They flew in all kinds of weather conditions and they flew at night. They made at least three takeoffs and landings per hour. While no major problems developed, minor difficulties associated with gear and flap motors and with some accessories were uncovered and corrected.

The North American Navion.

Originally dubbed the "Thunderbolt Amphibian" when it was announced in
1944, the SeaBee was an ambitious attempt by the President of Republic
Aviation, Fred Marchev, to substantially reduce the man-hours required to
build airplanes. His critics called it "Marchev's folly" . . . it turned out
they were right. Republic was forced to suspend production of the SeaBee
when it became obvious the projected costs were not within reach.

Bonanza production line, August, 1946. Twin Beech production line is in the background.

A high ranking priest performing an anointing ceremony on one of five Bonanzas that had just arrived at Don Muang Aerodrome, Bangkok, Siam. January, 1948.

It was determined that torsional vibration dampeners should be added to the engine to insure long engine life and low maintenance. This major design change Continental Motors cheerfully agreed to, but it delayed availability of engines until the first part of 1947. This time was put to good use. The Bonanza was already a quiet airplane, but additional research in soundproofing was conducted during the delay period. And improvements were made. Walter Beech was able to announce to those who had ordered Bonanzas that "the sound level in the cabin of the Bonanza is less than 1/20th the intensity of the sound level in the cabin of a competitive airplane that has a considerably lower cruising speed".

Anticipating a long production life for the Bonanza, the company spent over $600,000 developing precision "Class A" tooling. This type of tooling was expensive but it insured the closer tolerances necessary for a quality product. Quantities were provided to support a 16-unit-a-day production rate.

The company received 500 orders with cash deposits prior to release of specifications or any detailed information on the new Beechcraft, such was the reputation of Walter Beech. With the release of specifications the total grew to 1500 before the first Bonanza could be delivered. The intensive Bonanza test program continued through 1946 with production deliveries following type certification on March 25, 1947.

Production reached 12 units a day during 1947 and Bonanzas were soon showing their distinctive V-tails in faraway places. Its popularity was indeed world wide. Before the Bonanza had reached its second birthday there were an even dozen Maharajas flying their royal Bonanzas throughout their respective principalities in India. (It was rumored fear of revolution had some part in their selection of the speedy Bonanza.) Bonanzas became a familiar sight in South America, Europe, Asia, Africa, and the Middle East.

A 1947 look at a Franklin engine for the Bonanza. If this engine had been selected for production airplanes there would have been an A35F Bonanza.

Piper might have been in the all-metal, four-place market as early as 1947 with the Piper Skysedan. The one prototype that was built used a 165 horsepower engine and cruised at 140 MPH, had retractable conventional landing gear. Production was cancelled, probably because of the aviation recession of 1948-1949. The Bonanza's established dominance in the market may also have been a factor.

Its only direct competition was the North American Navion. The Navion, although a fine airplane, lacked the performance of the Bonanza and never really successfully challenged it, even after purchase of the design by Ryan. More and more horsepower was added to the Navion in an effort to match Bonanza performance. The outcome was always the same — with identical engines, the Bonanza was 25 MPH faster. There have been other, more recent challenges. The pressurized, single engine airplane that "was going to put the Bonanza out of business within two years" according to a quote attributed to the company president, experienced one of the shortest production runs in the history of general aviation.

*   *   *

The Bonanza has contributed mightily to other Beech designs. The first was the Beechcraft Model 45 Mentor, a military training plane that served a long and distinguished career as the basic trainer for both the Air Force and Navy. The tandem seat, two-place Mentor was derived from the basic Bonanza design with similar wings, landing gear and lower fuselage. Almost 80 percent of the Bonanza tooling was used in building the Mentor. The Bonanza design has contributed substantially to the development of virtually every airplane currently manufactured by Beech Aircraft. With the exception of the Musketeer, all other Beechcrafts incorporate Bonanza components.

The year 1970 marked the 25th anniversary of the Bonanza's first flight, and it celebrated the occasion by outselling all other single engine retractables, some costing half as much and all of them newer in design. What made it possible? Some will say a mystique has been created, either by Beech or Bonanza owners, around the design; a mystique which makes the Bonanza nearly self-perpetuating. There may be an element of truth in that charge. After all, the Bonanza is the only airplane in current production to have its own owner organization, the American Bonanza Society, some 3000 strong and growing. Membership in the Society includes owners of all models, from the 1947 Model 35 to the latest and most elaborately equipped V35B. And this may be at least part of the design's appeal. If you can afford to own an airplane, the chances are good you can afford a Bonanza. A used 24-year-old "straight" 35 can be purchased for as little as $6000; then you're stepping out in the "Cadillac" of the single engine fleet. A strong market for used Bonanzas of all models keeps the resale value up, and makes it that much easier for owners of the newer models to continue to trade their machine in on a brand new one every so often. Maybe it is self-perpetuating.

Bonanzas also lend themselves well to modification, so there is additional demand from those who enjoy this activity. In fact, many owners make a game of seeing how close they can get their earlier model to resemble a current offering. I know one who has put more hours into rebuilding a 1962 P35 Bonanza than were originally required for its complete manufacture. The design's long life encourages this emulation and Beech does provide improvement kits when the demand warrants it.

I believe, however, the Bonanza's amazing longevity is due more to an infrequent combination of design and manufacturing principles. The Bonanza's silhouette was strikingly different for light plane design in 1946, it's still uncommon today. As one long-time Beech dealer puts it, "Have you ever noticed? The man who owns a Bonanza almost always turns to look at it as he walks away." Then there is the engineering philosophy which dictated abundant internal structure and gave the Bonanza that "built to last forever" appearance. It's not likely to be duplicated with today's high tooling and fabricating costs. The manufacturing attention to detail can, and perhaps has been duplicated, but not often. In all-around performance the Bonanza has been approached, but never surpassed!

Today nearly 10,000 models of the V-tail classic have been manufactured and over 1800 of its conventional tailed cousins, the Models 33 and 36, visible proof of Walter Beech's "modern miracle of aeronautical design".

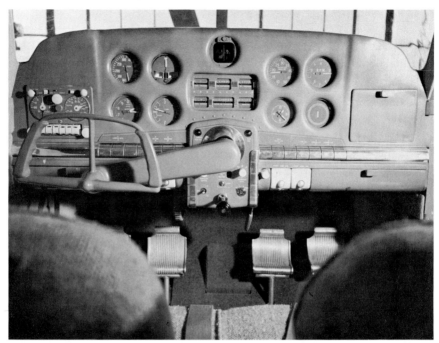

A mockup of the first Bonanza instrument panel.

The Bonanza panel today. The instruments in the center are modern vertical readout engine gages.

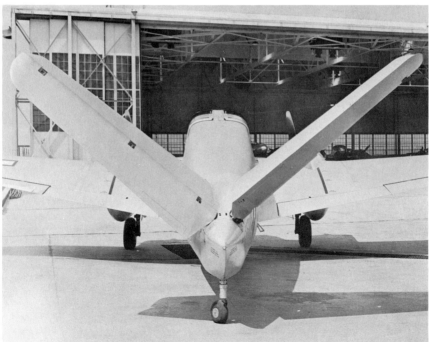

The first Beechcraft with a V-Tail, an experimental AT-10 (Beech Model 26).

29

More About The V-Tail

The Bonanza was the first airplane in quantity production to use the unusual and distinctive V-tail, but the origin of the design can be traced back to the 1930s. The following comments appeared in the March, 1932 issue of a publication titled "Aircraft Engineering."

"The Rudlicki Vee tail is the invention of M. Georges Rudlicki, Technical Director of E. Plage i T. Laskiewicz, the Polish aircraft constructors, in Lublin. This revolutionary arrangement of the tail surfaces offers several interesting advantages and overcomes some of the inconveniences of the conventional form of tail. For military aircraft it is particularly advantageous as it gives better visibility towards the rear and permits a gunner to defend himself better from the back. Requiring a smaller area to give the same effect as a normal tail it weighs 35 percent less and by consequent reduction of drag slightly increases the speed of an aeroplane. In wind tunnel experiments and in actual flight, it has proved to be at least as efficient as the conventional form."

Some aviation historians believe the V-tail was flown in England some 20 years prior to the Rudlicki application. In any event, its first appearance in the United States was on a glider designed and flown by a Mr. Robert Stanley during the late thirties.

New interest in a "V" configuration occurred with the higher speeds experienced during the latter part of World War II. The British company of Westland Aircraft Ltd. conducted wind tunnel tests in 1943, about the same time that Beech began their effort with the twin engine AT-10. Still later, Bell Aircraft flew the V-tail on a King Cobra for an Air Force evaluation. Bell concluded that if a V-tail were constructed with a total area equal to the total combined area of a conventional empennage, and the movable surfaces were the same, then the control effectiveness of the V-tail would be some 40 percent greater than the total control effectiveness of the conventional empennage. The Air Force flight test report, while admitting to some advantages for the arrangement, did not recommend adoption of the "V". Their investigation did, however, generally support the conclusions already reached by Beech and Bell.

Preproduction Bonanzas had fabric covered ruddervators as well as fabric covered flaps and ailerons. This approach was abandoned prior to production.

A 1947 look at dorsal fins for the Bonanza. They did nothing aerodynamically so the investigation was dropped.

Beech was not the only manufacturer with an interest in V-Tails. These are photographs of development work undertaken by Bell Aircraft during 1948.

The conventional tail appearing in the left of this picture probably belongs to a Bell King Cobra. The fuselage used for the V-Tail mockup shown here is also a P63 King Cobra fuselage. Note the large ventral fin.

The experimental V-Tailed RP-63G King Cobra taxiing in after a test flight, 1948. The ventral fin is visible under the left wing.

On the Bonanza, these advantages have been realized. A reduction in total tail area with the attendant reduction in drag and weight. Gordon calculated a weight savings of 11.6 pounds. The reduction in number of surface to fuselage intersections also contributes to a reduction in drag. Other flight advantages are better spin recovery and fewer trim changes with changes in power. With regard to spins, Beech flight tests indicate not only improved spin recovery but a resistance to spin entry. With the elevator full back there is less rudder power available to initiate a spin. Also, with the control wheel full back applying full rudder tends to unstall the airplane due to reduced elevator effectiveness.

Additional benefits are simplified manufacturing, tooling, and parts stocking, and reduced risk of ground damage from rocks thrown back by the wheels. In the practical world of the engineer it's unlikely they realized the unusual tail configuration would offer still another benefit perhaps as important as the others . . . it became a mark of distinction . . . identifying the finest airplane in its class!

Notice here the automatic trailing antenna mounted over V-Tail. Antenna reeled out at 110 MPH and reeled back in when airspeed dropped to 100 MPH. This arrangement was used until A35 D-1961. It was then replaced with a fixed antenna.

The Elevator Down Spring

All Bonanzas have an elevator down spring incorporated into the control system. Other Beechcrafts, such as the Super 18, have used down springs, and they are now beginning to show up in other manufacturers' airplanes. The down spring can best be described as a form of insurance for the unwary pilot, since it gives the airplane better pitch stability than it otherwise would have when loaded aft of the rear limits.

Visualize an airplane on final approach loaded well aft, actually out of the loading envelope. Elevator control pressures will be very light and sloppy. In this condition the elevator may very well be in a slight "down" position to keep the nose down and the airspeed up to approach speed. Should the airplane lose airspeed, either through the inattention of the pilot or turbulence, the trim tab will become less effective and allow the elevator to move up into a more trailing position. This in turn will allow the nose to come up, the airspeed to fall off still more, and the situation will continue to deteriorate unless corrective action is taken by the pilot. This condition is known as dynamic pitch instability.

Now visualize the same airplane on the same approach with an elevator down spring. The elevator trim tab is now trimmed against the pull of the down spring on the elevator. With a loss in airspeed and trim tab effectiveness the down spring takes over, pulling the elevator down, lowering the nose and increasing the airspeed until the forces exerted by the trim tab and down spring are once again in equilibrium, which will be the pilot's original trim speed.

34

Beech even considered the V-Tail for the Mentor trainer as evidenced by
this model.

Another Beechcraft with a V-Tail, the Model 1025 Cardinal Target System
used by air defense missile batteries.

Beechcraft
Model 34 Twin-Quad Transport

During and immediately following the war it was felt the Civil Aeronautics Board would encourage the development of an extensive network of feeder-line short-haul airlines. Beech Aircraft Corporation designed an airplane tailored to meet this need, the Model 34 twin-quad transport. It could carry 20 people and their baggage plus 1000 pounds of airmail or air express. It could clear a 50-foot obstacle in 2600 feet at sea level, cruise 180 MPH, and had a maximum range ability of 1400 miles with a 45-minute reserve.

The twin-quad was a unique design concept. Beech was interested in providing the lowest possible operating costs for the feederlines, yet also provide a high degree of safety and dependability. To meet the safety requirement the design group decided on four engines, but they were to be completely submerged in the leading edge of the wings, and would drive only two propellers. This configuration would give four-engine safety with twin-engine economy. The engines were mounted perpendicular to the thrust line and coupled in pairs through gear boxes. This arrangement reduced the danger from engine failure during takeoff, and at the same time overcame the piloting problem of feathering the propeller of a dead engine and trimming out the airplane. The dead engine withdrew immediately and automatically from the gear train, permitting the remaining live engine in the pair to continue driving the propeller.

With the engines completely submerged in the wings no frontal area drag was set up by exposed engines or nacelles. The flat engines buried in the wings gave a resultant aerodynamic efficiency approaching that of a high performance soaring plane. All antennas were buried, and of course the V-tail further contributed to a low drag profile.

An interesting safety feature was the structural keels built into the fuselage on both sides. The keels were designed to carry normal landing loads in a wheels-up position. An actual wheels-up test confirmed the usefulness of this feature.

During a test flight of the prototype on January 17, 1949, a small electrical fire occurred in the cabin just after takeoff. In the ensuing excitement, a crew member inadvertently turned off the emergency master switch and killed all four engines. Because of the low altitude, power could not be restored in time to avoid a forced landing in unsuitable terrain. With destruction of the prototype, and with the intended market not materializing, Beech abandoned plans to produce the airplane.

Twin-Quad "firsts"

— The first airplane in the world to use engines completely submerged in the wings.

— First to combine four engines with two propellers.

— First to have integral emergency landing keels on the bottom of the fuselage.

— First large airplane to use the V-tail.

It was the only high wing Beechcraft ever built and the only other commercial Beechcraft to use the V-tail.

Beechcraft Model 34 twin-quad transport (first flight, June, 1947).

Bonanza Integrity

Beech had an opportunity early in the production life of the Bonanza to prove he was standing behind his product. In spite of the extensive design work, testing and the controls used in the development and manufacture of the Bonanza, 250 of the first 800 units developed minor flaws that Walter Beech felt should be corrected. In a sense, the problem had been caused by the Bonanza's success.

Because of the rapid production build-up to meet demand, the Beech factory soon ran short of automatic riveting capacity. If production was to be maintained at a high rate, some other method had to be found to attach the wing skins to the stringers. Work was accomplished in the experimental shop with roll-welded skins and stringers and these were installed on test wings. Structural testing indicated they were every bit as good as the conventional riveted skins. There wasn't time however to extensively service test an airplane with these wings installed. 250 sets of wings were built in this manner.

Later periodic inspection of some of these airplanes revealed small and relatively insignificant cracks in the vicinity of some of the weld spots. The cracks were of no structural significance but they indicated these skins would not give the in-service life of the conventionally riveted skin. Beech Aircraft Corporation quickly notified all 250 owners of these Bonanzas, requesting that they bring their airplanes back to the factory for rework of both wings at no charge to them. By this action, Walter Beech demonstrated his keen devotion to product integrity.

Reworking wings, September, 1947.

Bevo Howard with the A35 Bonanza he used at Cleveland (1948).

An unusual display of Bonanza strength occurred during the 1948 National Air Races in Cleveland, Ohio. Famed aerobatic pilot, Beverly (Bevo) Howard put a stock Model A35 Bonanza (D-1601) through an impressive 10-minute show of aerobatics. His outstanding performance included slow rolls, a four-point roll followed by an eight-point roll, two inverted slow rolls, a Cuban-eight followed by slow roll, a snap roll in the top of a loop followed by a loop, inverted flight, and an Immelman followed by a snap roll. Although he didn't perform the maneuver at the air races, Bevo had, at the factory, dived the airplane in an inverted position to 205 MPH indicated, then pushed the stick forward to perform an outside loop. His show at Cleveland attracted more attention than any other stunt flying in the three-day National Air Races and greatly boosted the Bonanza's reputation as the strongest in its class.

Bonanza Dive Tests

During 1948 a series of unique remote controlled dive tests were conducted to prove out in actual flight the Bonanza's structural strength.

A radio remote control unit was borrowed from the Air Force and installed in Bonanza No. 4, the fourth pre-production experimental unit. A Model 18 Twin Beech was equipped with the transmitting components and used as the mother ship. The dive tests were conducted in an area approximately 10 miles south of the former Army Air Corps field at Herington, Kansas. Seven separate dive tests were made. The first test was witnessed by representatives of the Army, Navy, and the then CAA as well as Beech personnel.

The procedure for a typical dive test was to fly both airplanes to Herington with the Bonanza being flown by radio remote control from the Model 18. A company pilot would be in the Bonanza during the flight to monitor the systems. When the airplanes reached Herington, final adjustments would be made in preparation for the "Nullo" flight. This activity included addition of ballast to replace the pilot, adjustments of the cameras, VG recorder, etc.

"Nullo" takeoff by radio control was accomplished from the Model 18 which started its own takeoff run as the controlled airplane left the ground. The airplanes were flown in a climb together until the Bonanza reached 12,000 feet. The Twin Beech would remain somewhat lower. At this point the controlling pilot would give forward wheel by radio control and put the Bonanza into a steep dive. As the Bonanza gained speed the mother ship was put into a shallower dive in order to follow and observe. The Bonanza was held at maximum speed for several seconds and then pulled out of the dive and into level flight at about 5000 feet. The two airplanes would then return to Herington and the Bonanza inspected for any evidence of structural overload.

The first of these seven tests almost ended in disaster during the landing attempt. It was a typical Kansas day with the wind blowing from the south at 30 MPH with gusts up to 45 MPH. Eleven passes were made before a successful landing was accomplished. The airplane wanted to float, then suddenly it would drop, hit the runway hard, and be in the air again.

The maximum speed reached in these dives was 286 MPH indicated airspeed. The angle of dive was approximately 45 degrees. Maximum acceleration during pullout was 3.5 G's. The autopilot proved to be the limiting factor, this was the maximum control force it could exert. The speed increase in the dive from 200 MPH to 280 MPH took only six seconds, which confirmed the fact that the Bonanza was indeed a very aerodynamically clean airplane.

Although nothing as rigorous as these tests would occur during normal usage of the airplane they did serve to substantiate the Bonanza structure.

The tests also resulted in additional changes to the design which made it strong enough to license at full gross weight in the Utility Category. To meet these more stringent qualifications, an airframe must be at least 15.7 percent stronger structurally than Normal Category requirements.

Bonanza radio controlled drone used in dive tests.

Drone Bonanza in flight (picture taken from the mother ship, a Model 18 Twin Beech) August, 1948.

The Bonanza Landing Gear

It would be difficult to select any one feature of the Bonanza and rank it as its most outstanding. In any ranking, however, the landing gear would certainly be high up the list. Electrically operated, it has none of the maintenance and reliability problems associated with hydraulically operated gears with their maze of plumbing and pressure pumps.

With more than 14,000 of these landing gears in service today, it is easily the most thoroughly proven retractable landing gear in the world. The Bonanza gear is used on Beechcraft Barons, Travel Airs, Debonairs, and the Air Force and Navy Mentor. It was drop tested 20 feet per second (1200 feet per minute) to meet the Navy's simulated carrier landing requirements. In use on the Beechcraft E55 Baron it is supporting a 5300-pound airplane which is a good indication of the strength and growth potential designed into the original gear.

In the early days of the Bonanza it was thought by some in the industry that the nose gear was weak and wouldn't stand the punishment of rough field operation. Nothing could have been further from the truth. Actually what problems that did occur were the result of pilots inexperienced with tricycle gears taking Bonanzas into rough ground marginally suitable for conventional geared aircraft. As other tricycle geared airplanes appeared on the market, the Bonanza compared quite favorably with them in rough field service. The landing gear has, however, been strengthened and improved through the years to accommodate increases in gross weight.

Model 35 landing gear, June, 1946.

The landing gear used on the Beechcraft Mentor trainer was an improved version of the original Model 35 gear. This is the Mentor prototype with (from left to right) Walter Beech, Vice President and General Manager Jack Gaty, Test Pilot Vern Carstens, and Vice President of Engineering Ted Wells.

With a long wheel base of seven feet and a track of nine feet seven inches, the Bonanza was and still is the easiest airplane in its class to land. It also sets higher off the ground than other low-wing retractables thus reducing the float from ground effect yet retaining enough of it to "air cushion" landings. This additional height greatly reduces the possibility of damage to the airframe and propeller when taxiing over loose gravel.

In designing the tricycle gear for the Bonanza every attempt was made to conserve all the advantages of tricycle gear and eliminate the disadvantages which had appeared in some other tricycle geared airplanes of that time. In order to permit the airplane to take off quickly from soft fields the design incorporates a considerable angle of attack of the wing when the airplane is in a three-point position. This permits the wing to start its lifting action as soon as taxiing speed has been attained.

It is an excellent short field airplane. Due to the positioning of the nose wheel ahead of the power plant rather than directly under it, and also the location of the main gear, a considerably greater portion of the airplane weight is supported by the main gear than is usually found. This means greater braking power, especially during the early stages of a landing roll-out.

The main gear is tied to both the front and rear spar and is braced to absorb landing loads from all directions. The nose gear is equally well supported and is provided with an automatic centering device to head it down the runway in crosswind landings. All three gears are enclosed in flight by two doors each. On the main gear the outboard door is attached to the strut while the inboard operates in conjunction with the landing gear retract mechanism so as to be closed when the gear is either up or down. This prevents buffeting of the inboard door and damage to the mechanism by dirt and rocks when taxiing. It also smooths out the airflow when the gear is down on approach.

The original Model 35s had full swiveling nose wheels to take advantage of the tighter turning radius possible with this arrangement. A steerable version had actually been tried then abandoned in favor of steering by differential braking. Customer demand plus the necessity for nose wheel steering on ice and snow or when a brake failed caused Beech to use nose wheel steering on the A35 and after. Modification kits were provided for the earlier Model 35s and today virtually all of them have this feature.

Emergency manual extension is provided and consists of a collapsible hand crank just behind and between the two front seats. Approximately 50 turns counterclockwise serves to lower the gear. In the event the trouble is an electrical failure affecting the gear position lights a mechanical indicator just to the right of the pilot's rudder pedals will verify the gear position.

All Bonanzas are equipped with a landing gear safety switch on the right main gear shock strut. This switch is open when the weight of the aircraft has compressed the strut which is normally the case anytime it is on the ground. With the switch open, the landing gear cannot be raised. After takeoff the shock strut will drop down forcing the switch closed and completing the electrical circuit. The gear can then be raised. In addition to this safety device, which is designed to prevent retracting the gear while the airplane is on the ground, the Bonanza has a second safety feature to pre-

Beechcraft T-34B Navy Mentor in position for landing gear drop test.

vent landing with the gear up. It is a warning horn set to sound if the throttle is reduced to an "approach" power setting and the landing gear is still in the "up" position. This horn is triggered by a switch located on the throttle linkage.

In addition to these standard safety features, Beech offers on current production airplanes an option called the "Beechcraft Magic Hand". This system automatically lowers the gear on approach should you forget. By sensing both airspeed and throttle position the gear is automatically lowered when airspeed falls below 120 MPH and the throttle position is such that you are carrying twenty inches or less of manifold pressure. "Magic Hand" also incorporates a delayed retraction feature. The gear will not retract until the airplane has reached a speed of 90 MPH and there is at least twenty inches of manifold pressure. Here again sensing is from airspeed and throttle position. The idea is to delay retraction until there is sufficient speed and power to preclude any possibility of the airplane settling back to the runway after takeoff. The "Magic Hand" is available in kit form for retrofit on earlier model Bonanzas.

The Bonanza gear also serves as a highly effective air brake. The big wheels, shock struts, doors, and all the associated bracing and plumbing change the Bonanza in seconds to a totally different kind of airplane. The gear doors are heavily reinforced and designed to take exceptionally high gear extension speeds. Later models have normal gear extension speeds of 175 MPH indicated airspeed with a maximum permissible extension speed of 200 MPH. Thus rapid deceleration is possible by merely dropping the gear. The Bonanza can carry high pattern speeds in jet traffic and wait to dissipate that speed practically at the runway threshold.

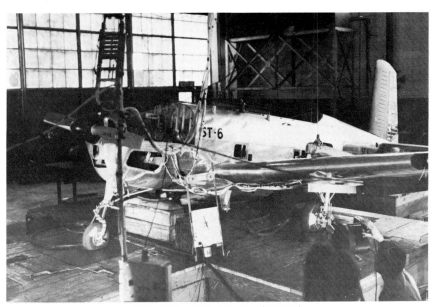

After drop. Only tires are damaged.

The Continental IO-520-B in a 1971 V35B Bonanza (note the heavily reinforced upper cowl door).

Power Plants

All production Bonanzas have been powered by six cylinder Continental engines. There is an FAA approved modification consisting of a 260 horsepower Lycoming conversion (by Rawdon of Wichita) however, few if any are in service today.

The E-165 was tailored by Continental for use in the Bonanza and it proved to be a good choice. The "E" series Continental grew right along with the Bonanza until it reached a peak output of 225 horsepower. The 1956 G35 was the last model to use this engine.

In 1957 the H35 Bonanza was introduced with an all-new, higher powered "O" series engine which developed 240 horsepower. This new engine had other benefits in addition to increased power. It was of wet sump configuration which meant for the first time there would be no external oil tank and oil lines. Also, it had provisions for a hydraulically controlled propeller. It had an automatic mixture control which completely eliminated manual leaning. The H35 Bonanza was the only model to ever have this feature. In 1958 the fuel injected Continental IO-470-C replaced the O-470-G. With the change to fuel injection Continental returned to manual mixture control.

The 1958 J35 Bonanza was the first mass produced, general aviation airplane to use fuel injection and thus introduced this advance to thousands of

46

pilots. For the first time, no possibility of carburetor ice. For the first time, scientific, accurate measurement of fuel to all cylinders for maximum power and economy. Fuel injection proved to be an outstanding success and all Bonanzas since 1958 have had it. Horsepower has grown from the 250 horsepower available on the "J", "K", and "M" models to the 260 horsepower of the "N" and "P" models and, with introduction of the IO-520-B Continental, 285 horsepower for the "S" and "V" series.

In contrast to the usual "bolted to the firewall" means of engine mounting all Bonanzas have employed a cradle type support for their power plants. This has resulted in an exceedingly vibration free engine support system.

Passenger Environment

Current model Bonanzas are known the world over for their outstanding cabin appointments and comfort levels. They are truly "living rooms in the sky" and few, if any, competitive makes of similar airplanes offer the same high degree of cabin environmental control.

This is true of today's Bonanzas, and it was certainly true of the first Bonanzas introduced to the public in 1947. Compared with the postwar offerings of other manufacturers, the Bonanza represented the greatest advance in small airplane comfort ever achieved.

To begin with, the cabin was designed for big people — six footers. In addition to having more head room than any other airplane then available, it featured two-position adjustable rudder pedals to accommodate different sized pilots. The copilot's rudder pedals will fold to the floor for complete stretch-out comfort (if dual brakes have not been added). The throw-over control column arrangement allows the front seat occupant who is not flying complete freedom of movement.

It is a wide cabin, a big 42 inches across in both front and back. The wisdom of building a cabin this size becomes apparent when you consider Beech is the only manufacturer that hasn't found it necessary to increase cabin width in this market during the last few years. The original 35 was 42 inches across, the current model is the same width.

The door is big, curving into the top of the cabin so you can step in and down rather than stooping. There's an entrance step. Few airplanes in the forties provided for easy entrance and exit for a woman. The Bonanza did, and with a step that retracted in flight along with the landing gear.

With noise level in an airplane bearing such a direct relationship to safety and comfort, a tremendous design and manufacturing effort went into making the Bonanza a very quiet airplane. Every bay in the fuselage has been analyzed for sound characteristics. Cabin sound level was reduced by a variety of methods. As a starter, additional structure was incorporated into the fuselage to eliminate the possibility of skin "canning" or "druming". The latest in special sound deadening materials were used and the windows and windshield are of extra thickness to silence air noise. Double blankets of fiber glass surround the cabin.

Good visibility was considered a prime requirement, not only for the pilot's convenience in congested areas but for passenger comfort. The designers were determined the feeling of claustrophobia that accompanied a ride in some planes would be absent. Windows were designed to begin well below shoulder level and extend up curving into the cabin ceiling so that it was possible to see almost straight up and down.

Ample ventilation was provided for both in flight and on the ground. The earlier Bonanzas have five fresh air vents, on later models this has been increased to eleven. After landing, the big rear windows can be opened for ground ventilation.

Visibility, even in the earliest model Bonanzas, is outstanding. Notice how the cabin windows extend well into the curvature of the cabin top.

Bonanza cabin, 1971.

The Bonanza as an Airliner

Included among its many firsts, the Bonanza has the distinction of being the first postwar single engine airplane to be operated as a feeder airline with regularly scheduled service for passengers, airmail and air express. On September 14, 1949, Central Airlines, Inc., Fort Worth, Texas, inaugurated a route through a four-state midwest area that included stops at 25 major cities. The airline fleet consisted of 11 new A35 Beechcraft Bonanzas. Keith Kahle, then president and general manager of Central Airlines stated, "We believe the Bonanza's record of dependability, performance and comfort as proved by the records covering more than 300,000,000 passenger miles flown to date in these Beechcrafts, will permit Central Airlines to offer its passengers a long needed feeder airline service equal in every way to the kind of scheduled air travel they receive on other skyways."

Central Airlines A35 Bonanza, 1949.

The Beechcraft Service Clinic

In the spring of 1949 Beech began a new factory "after sale service" program unique in aviation history. Primarily directed at Bonanza owners, it was later expanded to include other Beechcrafts. The Beechcraft Customer Service Clinic was held once a year at Dealer facilities around the country and the cost absorbed by the Beech factory and sponsoring Dealer organization.

At the Clinic, each Bonanza brought in received a thorough inspection by factory experts at no cost to the customer. The entire airplane was given a complete going over by service engineers who year after year looked at thousands of Bonanzas. In many, many cases they were able to save owners money by finding items in need of preventive maintenance, before replacement became necessary. In addition, the owner had an opportunity to pick up valuable operational information that often increased the utility of his aircraft and his ability to obtain the performance designed into it.

In recent years few new maintenance items were uncovered at Clinic Inspections, and the Beechcraft Service Clinic has been discontinued. Beechcraft Certified Service Stations now largely perform this function in routine annual inspections.

The factory did, however, derive benefit from the vast accumulation of knowledge from these inspections, knowledge that was used in the design of newer and even better Bonanzas.

Captain Bill Odom and the Waikiki Beech.

"Testifying in the most effective manner possible to the ability of the American aviation industry to produce aircraft and ideas of dramatic character, I invite your attention to the recent feat of Captain Bill Odom in accomplishing the greatest non-stop flight while using a Beechcraft Bonanza . . ."

Glenn L. Martin, 1949

Bonanza Long Distance Flights

CAPT. BILL ODOM AND THE WAIKIKI BEECH

Beechcrafts and their predecessors, the Travel Airs, made a habit of establishing and breaking distance and speed records. The first postwar attempt to establish a new record was made by Capt. Bill Odom in a Model 35 Bonanza, called the "Waikiki Beech".

Odom was a midwesterner, born in Porum, Oklahoma, and brought up in Kansas City, Missouri. His start in aviation was as a weather forecaster for a major airline. In his spare time he learned to fly and then sold airplanes on the side. During the war he gained considerable long distance navigational experience by delivering bombers to England and later flew the "hump" route between India and China. It was with the confidence gained from this background that he established two new world records for long distance flying, both in the same Bonanza.

The first record was actually an aborted attempt to establish the second. On January 12, 1949, Odom departed Hickam Field, Honolulu for a non-stop flight to Teterboro, New Jersey. After successfully crossing the Pacific, he encountered severe weather in the vicinity of Reno, Nevada, and was forced to return to the West Coast where he landed at Oakland just 22 hours and 6 minutes after departing Hawaii. The flight did serve to set a record. Odom

The Waikiki Beech made both trips westbound on wings other than her own. This picture was taken at Oakland prior to first record attempt. The transport is a Pan American Airways DC-4.

53

took the non-stop distance record for Bonanza category away from the Russians who had held it for over 12 years. It was also the first light plane flight between Hawaii and the U. S. mainland. The great circle distance covered was 2406.9 miles but Odom actually flew 2900 miles.

Odom's most famous flight was to occur nearly two months later on March 7, when he again departed from runway 8 at Hickam Field, in the same Bonanza, and successfully flew the distance of 4957 miles to Teterboro, New Jersey, thus setting a new world record for non-stop distance flying for all light airplanes, not only in the Bonanza category, (those weighing from 2204.7 to 3858 pounds) his record exceeded the mark for all other light plane categories as well. The Waikiki Beech was in the air for 36 hours and 2 minutes. Both flights were sponsored by Beech Aircraft Corporation and emphasized as a test of the Bonanza's efficiency and dependability . . . in contrast to distance flights of the prewar era, which were often more accurately described as daredevil ventures. Statistics of the Honolulu to Teterboro flight are impressive.

Takeoff weight . . . . 3858 pounds
Average ground speed (distance flown) . . . . 146.3 MPH
Average miles per gallon (distance flown) . . . . 19.37 MPG
Average gallons per hour . . . . 7.56 GPH
Fuel carried . . . . 288 gallons
Fuel used . . . . 272.25 gallons
Remaining . . . . 15.75 gallons
Oil carried . . . . 7.5 gallons
Oil used . . . . 1.5 gallons
Remaining . . . . 6.0 gallons
Distance over water . . . . 2474 miles
Distance over land . . . . 2799 miles
Total distance actually flown . . . . 5273 miles
Accredited great circle distance . . . . 4957 miles
Extra distance possible on fuel remaining . . . . 372 miles
Total cost of gas and oil $75.00

In addition to breaking all light plane distance records, Odom's flight came within 191 miles of equalling the longest single leg between refuelings (5464 miles) of the non-stop, round the world flight of a U. S. Air Force B-50, made February 26 through March 3. Without question, his flight demonstrated to the American public the efficiency, dependability and sophistication of the Beechcraft Bonanza.

Although both flights were made in 1949, when the later Model A35 Bonanza was already being manufactured, Odom's airplane was actually a straight Model 35, the fourth Bonanza manufactured. The airplane was almost three years old and during that time had been used by the engineering department on a large amount of test flying and development work. It was, in fact, the same Bonanza that had been test dived by radio remote control to indicated airspeeds of 286 miles per hour, with true airspeeds in excess of 300 miles per hour. The only modifications to the airplane were those necessary to install cabin fuel tanks holding 126 gallons, and two wing tip tanks holding 62 gallons each.

The Waikiki Beech also carried 7.5 gallons of oil. Even though 50 percent over gross, takeoff distance was still less than 3000 feet. Rate of climb at this weight was about 400 feet per minute. In an explanation of Bonanza efficiency, Ted Wells calculated that if an all-out effort were made with the Bonanza, with reduced margins of safety and performance, it actually had the capability of flying over 8000 miles non-stop.

After a nation-wide tour by Capt. Bill Odom, the Waikiki Beech was put on display in the Smithsonian Institution. Its famous pilot was killed, only six months after setting his record flight. On September 5, 1949, in one of the last of the postwar Cleveland Air Races, Odom's P-51 Mustang encountered the prop wash of another fighter and rolled into the ground.

From left to right, Capt. Bill Odom, Beech engineers Jerry Gordon, Herman Barnett, Noel Naidenoff, and Al Clark. 1949. Two sets of wing tip tanks were manufactured. This picture shows first set with visible weld seams.

Bill Odom on arrival at Teterboro, New Jersey. March, 1949.

55

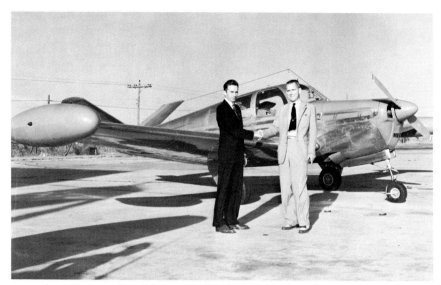

Congressman Mack (dark suit) with Jack Gaty, then Vice President and General Manager of Beech. October, 1951.

Congressman Peter F. Mack, Jr. and the Friendship Flame.

The Waikiki Beech was removed from the Smithsonian Institution in 1951 and loaned to Congressman Peter F. Mack, Jr., for an around-the-world flight. Congressman Mack renamed the plane the "Friendship Flame" and on October 7 took off from Springfield, Illinois for a 113-day, 33,000-mile goodwill tour of 45 major cities in 35 countries.

Bonanza number 4, then the oldest Bonanza still flying and the second flying model built, returned to Wichita from Mack's goodwill tour April 19, 1952. Today it is stored in a warehouse at the Beech facility in Salina, Kansas.

Here is the Waikiki Beech as she appeared at the time of this writing. Old "Number 4" has not felt the air under her wings for 18 years.

56

MARION L. (PAT) BOLING AND THE
PHILIPPINE BONANZA

On July 31, 1958, Capt. Pat Boling departed Manila in the Philippines and established a new non-stop, long distance solo flight record of 6856 miles, landing in Pendleton, Oregon on August 1, 1958.

Like Odom's venture, Boling's trip was sponsored by Beech Aircraft Corporation. He flew in an especially equipped J-35 Bonanza, D-5650. Odom's wing tip fuel tanks were used. The airplane also had the standard two 25-gallon inboard wing tanks, plus two 31-gallon outboard auxiliary wing tanks and three interconnected fuselage tanks holding a total of 162 gallons. Total fuel capacity was 402 gallons. Although the airplane was built up from a standard J-35 Bonanza, sections of the Model 95 wing were used so the larger 31-gallon Travel Air auxiliary tanks could be installed. An auxiliary oil tank was also included and held five extra gallons.

The Philippine Bonanza was well equipped for the trip. Warning horns would sound if the plane deviated from predetermined altitudes or airspeeds, and an alarm would sound every hour unless reset by the pilot. In addition to

Pat Boling on arrival at Pendleton, Oregon. August 1, 1958.

auto-pilot and high frequency radio equipment, it had an 18-hour supply of oxygen, a small electric percolator and an electric shaver which could be plugged into the cigarette lighter receptacle. A vibrator pillow was also carried to ease strain during the long confinement.

Like Odom, Pat Boling was originally from the middle west. He was born in Eddy, Oklahoma, September 7, 1914. His experience for the trip was considerable. After winning his wings in the U. S. Navy, he joined United Airlines in 1941 and rose to the position of captain on transcontinental flights in DC-7s from San Francisco to New York. Boling had stood on Honolulu Airport that night on March 7, 1949, when Bill Odom took off for New York. He resolved then and there to someday beat Odom's record.

In 1957, Boling advised Beech he was interested in buying a Bonanza to attempt a new long-distance record with the backing of some of his friends. Jack Gaty, who had backed Odom's flights in 1949, decided Boling was the man to set a new record and the Beech factory should again back the attempt. It had been nine years since a record had been set and a new success would serve as dramatic proof of the even greater efficiency and reliability of the latest model Bonanza. The flight did just that.

```
Total distance actually flown ..................... 7090 miles
Official great circle route distance .............. 6856 miles
Over water ....................................... 6555 miles
Over land ........................................ 535 miles
Extra distance possible on remaining fuel .......... 253 miles
Total value of gas and oil used ................... $139.85
Total time ....................................... 45:43 hours
Takeoff weight ................................... 4964 lbs.
Normal gross weight .............................. 2900 lbs.
Average ground speed (actual distance) ............ 155 MPH
Average gallons per hour (actual distance) ......... 8.55 GPH
Total gas carried ................................ 402 gallons
Total gas used ................................... 391 gallons
Total gas remaining .............................. 11 gallons
```

The flight was a tremendous success, but the distance flown was actually short of expectations. Manila had been selected as a starting point to give the Bonanza more land to cover at the end of the trip. (Odom could have gone even farther had there been a place to land east of New York.) It was hoped that with some favorable tail winds Boling might reach Wichita, Kansas. The tail winds failed to develop, however, and in addition he encountered icing in the area of the Queen Charlotte Islands which may have frozen over a fuel tank vent, causing some siphoning-off of fuel. The trip did accomplish the objective of proving the superiority of the latest model Bonanza and Continental's new 250 horsepower, fuel-injected engine.

Beech has not sponsored any long-distance attempts since the Boling flight and it is unlikely it will in the future. Beech officials now feel long range distance attempts are becoming more a matter of endurance of the pilot. The reliability and performance of the modern day airplane has been proven.

Peter Gluckmann and the Philippine Bonanza.

The Philippine Bonanza remained at the Beech factory and was used for various shows and exhibits until January of 1960. At that time Peter Gluckmann approached Mrs. Beech with an offer to buy the aircraft. German-born Gluckmann, a San Francisco watch-maker, had made numerous long-distance flights in his own older model Bonanza and was interested in breaking Boling's record in N35U. Beech elected not to sponsor Gluckmann but did agree to sell him the airplane complete with all the tanks but less the engine.

Still more fuel tanks and a new 260 horsepower Continental engine were installed. A larger 86-inch diameter propeller was used and the engine was allowed to turn 2800 RPM for takeoff. Estimated takeoff power was boosted to 275 horsepower. The airplane, together with the rather large Gluckmann and all the fuel, grossed out at 6020 pounds. Jerry Gordon calculated that at this weight the rate of climb (gear up) would be close to zero.

Gluckmann's plan was to depart from Hong Kong, reach the United States, and fly inland as far as his fuel would take him. With the additional tanks, he estimated he had fuel for a total of 60 hours flying. Hong Kong was chosen both for the distance and because it had a long 8350-foot runway running directly out to sea. Aero Jet-General Jato units were to be used for the takeoff. The departure from Hong Kong went as planned (except only one Jato bottle was used, the igniter for the other having been stolen). Gluckmann used 6000 feet of runway and actually had the airplane flying before firing his rocket. Sixteen hours out he encountered a severe weather front and was forced to return. He elected to land at Tokyo.

On April 27, 1960 he departed Tokyo (without Jato assist) for New York. He was 7½ hours out when last heard from by a U. S. Coast Guard vessel between Tokyo and Midway Island. The famous Philippine Bonanza and its last pilot rest somewhere at the bottom of the Pacific.

The Philippine Bonanza.

Opening of the first annual American Bonanza Society meeting, June 26, 1969. The meeting was held in the Walter H. Beech Hall at the Beech factory.

Dr. B. J. McClanahan (on the right) discussing with the author the unusually large attendance at the first Bonanza Society meeting.

The American Bonanza Society

Early in 1967 Dr. B. J. McClanahan took the first steps to form a Society of Bonanza owners to:

"promote and encourage interest in the operation and maintenance of single engine Bonanza aircraft and to collect from and disseminate to the members ideas, experiences and data in relation to such aircraft and the safe flying of the same";

"to cultivate and promote friendship and sociability among the members".

He has succeeded admirably. As of this writing the American Bonanza Society has 3000 members. It is the first such organization formed around an aircraft design still in current production.

On June 26, 1969 the Society opened its first annual meeting in Wichita, Kansas at the home of the Beechcraft Bonanza. Attendance during the three-day meeting approached 700. The nearly 300 Bonanzas parked at Wichita Municipal Airport created a rare display of the design's numbers and longevity.

Membership in the American Bonanza Society is open to anyone "interested in the objects and purposes of the corporation". The National Headquarters address is:

The American Bonanza Society
Chemung County Airport
Horseheads, New York 14845

During the meeting several member Bonanzas were on exhibit outside the Walter H. Beech Hall. Pictured here is one of the most modified Bonanzas in the world, a 1948 Model 35 owned by Bill Squires. Arrival of the aircraft was occasion for a number of Beechcrafters who helped build it to get together for a picture. From left to right, Herman Barnett, Bill Squires, Merle Leroux, Glenn Hetrick, O. M. Weldon, Earl Smith, W. C. Jackson, A. R. Lepley, H. L. Hays, Larry Baird, Glenn Ehling, H. J. Agnew, H. S. Gregory, V. E. Fisher, and J. N. Colvin.

Members honored during the Wichita meeting were Dr. Francis X. Sommer, Barbourville, Kentucky, Dr. Hypolite T. Landry, Jr., Baton Rouge, Louisiana, James W. Gardner, Tyrone, Pennsylvania, and Bill Guinther, Kutztown, Pennsylvania.

Dr. Sommer with Dr. John Rieger flying as copilot set three new class speed records during their around-the-world trip in his S35 Bonanza. The records were for flying time from New York to Paris, Tokyo to Point Barrow, Alaska, and Point Barrow to New York. The doctors' trip began May 19, 1967 to commemorate the 40th anniversary of Charles Lindbergh's New York to Paris flight.

Dr. Hypolite T. Landry (using Dr. Sommer's fuselage tanks) circled the globe during May, 1969 in his S35 Bonanza and captured the around-the-world speed record for his class. In the process he also set 13 new international speed records.

James W. Gardner and his V35 were honored for placing first for three consecutive years as best aircraft in the single engine class at the Reading Air Show.*

Bill Guinther (not pictured) flew a standard Model 36 Bonanza in the 1969 London Daily Mail Air Race and won "The Most Meritorious American Entry Prize" of $12,000. His Model 36 was equipped with two 80-gallon fuselage fuel tanks mounted in the rear seat area. Time from London to New York was 22 hours, 13 minutes.

---

*Bill Squires' modified Model 35 Bonanza placed second behind James Gardner's Bonanza at the 1969 Reading Show. In 1970, their roles were reversed. Squires won first place, Gardner second.

From left to right, Dr. Francis X. Sommer, Dr. Hypolite T. Landry, Jr., Bill Squires, and James W. Gardner. In the background is Dr. Sommer's record setting Bonanza.

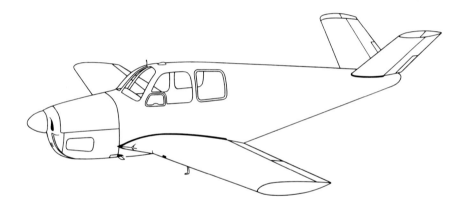

The Bonanza Models

Here we will cover, with as much detail as possible, every model of the Bonanza as it was delivered from the factory.

Since the Bonanza has been the modification buff's dream project through the years, it is unlikely any of the early airplanes are still in the original factory configuration. Sooner or later almost every Bonanza falls into the hands of an aficionado who will try to make it as much like a new production unit as is humanly possible. It can't be done, of course, but many owners have come close to duplicating at least the external appearance of a fresh-off-the-line, current model. Beech has helped by making available numerous improvement kits when demand has warranted it.

Realizing the pitfalls then, we will describe every model as it rolled out the doors at Wichita, Kansas. Many of the changes that occurred during the production run of each model are also listed. Some of these changes are major, some very minor in nature. The small changes are included for three reasons. They may be of significance to some readers, they make the record more complete, and frankly it is sometimes difficult to draw a line between what is important and what is not. A reader contemplating purchase of a used S35 Bonanza, for example, will probably find all of the changes listed there of interest.

Generally, unless otherwise noted, each succeeding model will include the features of the prior model. Performance data is repeated, however, even though it may not have changed from the previous model. This was done so it would not be necessary to refer back to an earlier model or models to obtain a complete set of numbers. Where performance has changed it is called to your attention in the text.

All performance figures are at full gross weight, standard day. A minor reduction in factory listed performance between models with the same engine is usually caused by an increase in gross weight. Where gross weight has increased with no reduction in performance (with the same engine) several explanations could apply. The decrease was hardly measurable, there was a small offsetting aerodynamic cleanup, or the average performance of production airplanes was better than originally anticipated.

Minor range variations occur between some models with the same engine, gross weight, and fuel capacity because of a difference in altitude and speed used by the factory to calculate maximum range, or a difference in what is considered to be usable fuel. Beginning with the 1961 N35 Bonanza ranges are shown with an allowance for a reserve.

For their historical value we have included fly-away-factory base prices, including any price changes that occurred during the production run.

The information presented in this section of the book should not be used in lieu of the appropriate Bonanza owner's manual.

35

BONANZA
MODEL YEARS 1947, 1948

Top speed at sea level.................................184 MPH
Maximum recommended cruise power................62.5% (115.5 HP)
Cruise speed at 62.5% power at 10,000 feet (optimum altitude)
    full throttle, 2050 RPM..............................175 MPH
Standard fuel capacity ....40 gallons
Maximum range (at 165 MPH at 10,000 feet)
    with standard tanks........................750 miles, no reserve
    with 20-gallon fuselage auxiliary tank
        (60 gallons total)...................1100 miles, no reserve
Gross weight ....2550 pounds
Empty weight ....1558 pounds
Useful load ....992 pounds
Weight available for people and baggage, standard tanks full...730 pounds
Stall speed (landing, full flaps)............................55 MPH
Rate of climb at sea level........................950 feet per minute
Service ceiling ....18,000 feet
Airspeed limits Maneuvering ....130 MPH
               Maximum structural cruising ....160 MPH
               Never exceed ....202 MPH
               Flaps extended ....100 MPH
               Landing gear extended ....100 MPH
Fuel ....80/87 octane minimum

Commonly called the "straight 35", this Bonanza was the first of the line. Manufactured during 1947 and 1948, the production run included serials D-1 through D-1500. Fifteen hundred Bonanzas, more units than any later model.

The engine was the Continental E-165 which developed 165 horsepower at 2050 RPM (maximum continuous). It was originally intended the engine would turn no faster to insure the quietest possible cabin and maximum propeller efficiency. During production, however, takeoff RPM was increased to 2300 RPM to provide 185 horsepower for one minute.*

Aside from being a revolutionary new design, the Model 35 was the first medium priced airplane to offer complete night flying equipment together with low frequency radio and instrumentation for IFR flight as standard equipment. Wiring and switches were even incorporated into the standard airplane for flares, just in case the owner might later decide he wanted to install them.

Though few will be seen in service today, the original propeller was of laminated wood with a metal covered leading edge. Often referred to as a paddle prop it had a large profile, a diameter of 88 inches, and was a Beech design (R203). It was electrically controlled but not governed in the original version. Two 20-gallon internal wing tanks provided standard fuel capacity. The range of many of the original 35s and later models has been increased by installation of a 10- or 20-gallon baggage compartment tank. Wing tip tanks are also now available for an additional increase in range.

---

*D-1 thru D-491 were delivered with Continental E-165-4 or E-165-4A engines. These engines were later redesignated as E-185-1 Continentals to permit the higher RPM and horsepower.

THESE CHANGES OCCURRED DURING PRODUCTION:

Bonanzas D-1 through D-40 had fabric covered ailerons and flaps; D-41 and after the ailerons and flaps were changed to magnesium.

Redesign of the cabin door for improved operation, D-139, D-152 and after.

Front seat backs modified for limited angular adjustment with set screws, D-151 and after.

Landing gear visual indicator lighted, D-151 and after.

Additional cabin cold air provided, D-101 and after.

Reinforced wing walk trailing edge, D-839 and after.

Baggage tie-down straps added, D-839 and after.

Fuselage (baggage compartment) auxiliary tank made available as factory installed optional equipment, D-533 and after.

Individual rear seat belts, D-840 and after.

Battery box recessed in the firewall, D-1117 and after.

Flap gap doors discontinued with D-1078 because of negligible value and high maintenance (most of those installed have now been removed).

Optional engine priming system, D-1225 and after.

The factory suggested selling price was $7,975 for D-1 through D-973. For serials D-974 through D-1500 it was $8,945.

It is estimated approximately 600 of this model are still in service. The amazing longevity of this 24-year-old aircraft is in part responsible for a significant inspection Airworthiness Directive against it. The front tubular steel center section truss has been found cracked on some aircraft. Crystallization in the welds is believed to be a factor and this can be attributed to age.

Many or perhaps most of the Model 35s in service today have been modified with the Beech aluminum truss kit or one of the other FAA approved modifications now available. For those units still not modified the front truss must be inspected every 100 hours. An inspection of the rear tubular steel truss is required every 1000 hours on all of the Model 35 Bonanzas.

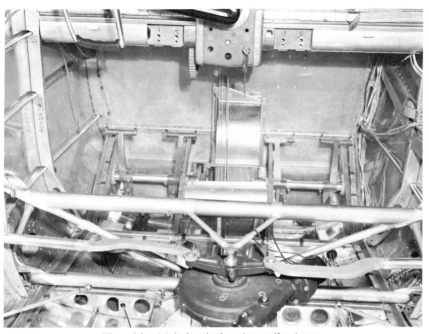

View of front tubular steel center section truss.

Walter Beech (on the left) and Bonanza serial D-1000. Notice the beautiful finish of the wood "paddle prop."

A35

BONANZA

Top speed at sea level . . . . 184 MPH

Maximum recommended cruise power . . . . 62.5% (115.5 HP)

Cruise speed at 62.5% power at 10,000 feet
    (optimum altitude) full throttle, 2050 RPM . . . . 173 MPH

Standard fuel capacity . . . . 40 gallons

Maximum range (at 165 MPH at 10,000 feet)
    with standard tanks . . . . 750 miles, no reserve
    with 20-gallon fuselage auxiliary tank
        (60 gallons total) . . . . 1100 miles, no reserve

Gross weight . . . . 2650 pounds

Empty weight . . . . 1580 pounds

Useful load . . . . 1070 pounds

Weight available for people and baggage, standard tanks full . . . 817 pounds

Stall speed (landing, full flaps) . . . . 56 MPH

Rate of climb at sea level . . . . 890 feet per minute

Service ceiling . . . . 17,100 feet

Airspeed limits Maneuvering . . . . 130 MPH
               Maximum structural cruising . . . . 160 MPH
               Never exceed . . . . 202 MPH
               Flaps extended . . . . 105 MPH
               Landing gear extended . . . . 125 MPH

Fuel . . . . 80/87 octane minimum

This was the first model Bonanza to be licensed at full gross weight in the utility category.

A popular early Bonanza because it was the first model to incorporate a conventional sheet metal center section carry-through structure for the wings. The A35 was the 1949 version and included serials D-1501 through D-2200 (and D-15001*) for a total of 701 units. The engine was the Continental E-185-1, the same used in the Model 35. Gross weight, however was increased and this is reflected in the slight decay in cruise speed, climb, and ceiling. The propeller was the plastic covered Beech B 200, diameter, 88".

NEW A35 FEATURES AND CHANGES:

Wing revisions to increase strength for higher gross weight and certification in the utility category at full gross.

An increase in the structural capacity of the baggage compartment to 270 pounds.

Useful load up 78 pounds.

Quickly removable rear seats.

Maximum gear down speed increased from 105 MPH to 125 MPH.

Gear retraction time decreased from 15.4 seconds to 11.5 seconds.

Maximum flap down speed increased from 100 MPH to 105 MPH.

A 33 amp hour battery (rather than the 25 amp hour battery used in the Model 35).

Turn and bank indicator electrically powered.

Optional complete exterior paint.

Coat hanger rod installed in the baggage compartment.

Bottom surface contour of elevator trim tab changed for increased effectiveness (airfoil shape).

Nosewheel made steerable. (Full swiveling had been fine until ice, snow, or a brake failure was encountered.)

THESE CHANGES OCCURRED DURING PRODUCTION:

A more powerful starter (Eclipse E-80) D-1823, D-1950 and after.

Optional fuel boost pump offered, D-1875 and after.

Flight Research electric propeller governor offered as an option, D-1581 and after.

Automatic trailing antenna replaced with fixed antenna, D-1961 and after.

Optional evaporative type air conditioner, D-2078 and after.

Increased takeoff horsepower, D-2141 and after.

The price of the A35 Bonanza was $9,445 until unit D-1943 at which time it was increased to $10,975.

*D-15001 was an "extra" airplane built for experimental flight test. It was given this unusual serial number by engineering because it was felt this number would never be reached and needed during the production life of the Bonanza. Only one other Bonanza, a G35 (D-15002) was numbered in this manner. This numbering system was abandoned and all other engineering prototypes have regular production serials.

B35

BONANZA

Top speed at sea level. . . . . .184 MPH
Maximum recommended cruise power. . . . . .62.5% (115.5 HP)
Cruise speed at 62.5% power at 10,000 feet (optimum altitude)
    full throttle, 2050 RPM. . . . . .173 MPH
Standard fuel capacity. . . . . .40 gallons
Maximum range (at 165 MPH at 10,000 feet)
    with standard tanks. . . . . .750 miles, no reserve
    with 20-gallon fuselage auxiliary tank
      (60 gallons total). . . . . .1100 miles, no reserve
Gross weight . . . . .2650 pounds
Empty weight . . . . .1575 pounds
Useful load . . . . .1075 pounds
Weight available for people and baggage, standard tanks full. . . 822 pounds

Stall speed (landing, full flaps) . . . . .56 MPH
Rate of climb at sea level . . . . .890 feet per minute
Service ceiling . . . . .17,100 feet

Airspeed limits Maneuvering . . . . 130 MPH
                Maximum structural cruising . . . . 160 MPH
                Never exceed . . . . 202 MPH
                Flaps extended . . . . 105 MPH
                Landing gear extended . . . . 125 MPH
Fuel . . . . .80/87 octane minimum

Manufactured during 1950, the B35 started with serial D-2201 and ended with serial D-2680, a total of 480 units. No major structural changes were included in this model but there was an improvement in horsepower available for takeoff. The engine used to power the B35 was the Continental E-185-8, which was allowed to turn 2450 RPM on takeoff for one minute. This resulted in 196 horsepower. Otherwise, maximum continuous power was unchanged. For that reason performance remained substantially the same as the A35.

OTHER NEW B35 FEATURES AND CHANGES:

Still faster gear retraction time, decreased from 11.5 seconds to 9.7 seconds.

Gear extension time decreased from 9.0 seconds to 7.4 seconds.

Flap travel increased from 20 degrees to 30 degrees.

Flap extension time decreased from 17.0 seconds to 11.2 seconds.

Flap retraction time decreased from 12.5 seconds to 7.2 seconds.

Wing tip navigation light indicators.

Oil cap access door in cowling.

Front and rear armrests.

Map pockets.

VHF radio transmitter.

New safety control wheel (flat, to absorb impact loads during a crash landing).

The price of the B35 was $11,975.

C35

BONANZA
MODEL YEARS 1951, 1952

Top speed at sea level . . . . 190 MPH

Maximum recommended cruise power . . . . 65% (120 HP)

Cruise speed at 65% power at 10,300 feet (optimum altitude)
full throttle, 2150 RPM . . . . 178 MPH

Standard fuel capacity . . . . 40 gallons

Maximum range (at 165 MPH at 10,000 feet)
with standard tanks . . . . 775 miles, no reserve
with 20-gallon fuselage auxiliary tank
(60 gallons total) . . . . 1180 miles, no reserve

Gross weight . . . . 2700 pounds

Empty weight . . . . 1647 pounds

Useful load . . . . 1053 pounds

Weight available for people and baggage, standard tanks full . . . 800 pounds

Stall speed (landing, full flaps) . . . . 55 MPH

Rate of climb at sea level . . . . 1100 feet per minute

Service ceiling . . . . 18,000 feet

Airspeed limits Maneuvering . . . . 130 MPH
Maximum structural cruising . . . . 160 MPH
Never exceed . . . . 202 MPH
Flaps extended . . . . 105 MPH
Landing gear extended . . . . 125 MPH

Fuel . . . . 80/87 octane minimum

74

Of the very early Bonanzas, the C35 is most often sought after because of the many important improvements made in this model. It had a long production run, beginning in late 1950 and extending through 1951 and 1952. Serials are from D-2681 through D-3400 except D-3293, which was destined to become a prototype of the E35 Bonanza. Total number of C35s built . . . 719.

To begin with, the C35 had more power. It was still an "E" series Continental but with another new "dash" number. The E-185-11 turned 2600 RPM and developed 205 horsepower on takeoff for one minute. Maximum continuous power was increased from the 165 horsepower available on all previous models to 185 horsepower at 2300 RPM. In conjunction with the increase in power a new propeller, the all metal 88-inch diameter Beech series 215 was used. The next biggest single change was in the tail of the C35. The chord (width) of the V-tail was increased 20 percent and the angle of incidence changed from 30 degrees to 33 degrees (as measured from the horizontal). This was done to improve directional stability and reduce yawing tendencies.

With the increase in power almost everything went up . . . speed, rate of climb, ceiling, and of course both the gross weight and empty weight. Useful load actually decreased 22 pounds.

OTHER NEW C35 FEATURES AND CHANGES:

Wing root fillets for a lower stall speed (even though gross weight was up, stall speed was reduced one mile per hour).

Wing structural changes for local beef-ups.

Separate fuel tank selector and wobble pump.

Additional landing gear circuit (sounded warning horn if switch was moved to "up" position when the weight of the aircraft was on the wheels).

Dual door lock.

Shoulder harnesses.

Rear seat headrest.

Adjustable rear seat back (two positions).

35 amp generator in place of 25 amp.

Safe flight stall warning horn and light (previously only a stall warning light had been used).

Improved instrument lighting.

Exterior paint standard.

Radio speaker moved forward and combined with dome light.

VHF radio transmitter and receiver standard equipment.

Improved cabin ventilation.

A flight of seven C35 Bonanzas ready for departure to Brazil (1951).

THESE CHANGES OCCURRED DURING PRODUCTION:

A further increase in cabin fresh air ventilation, D-3189 and after.

Improved cabin heat distribution, D-3351 and after.

The C35 Bonanza was the first commercial business aircraft to include a shoulder harness as standard equipment. This was done after exhaustive tests by Beech and the study of data of research institutions convinced them of the value of the harness in any crash landing.

The price of the C35 began at $12,990 but inflation created by the Korean War caused this price to be increased to $15,990 and still later to $18,990.

BONANZA

Top speed at sea level ....190 MPH

Maximum recommended cruise power ....75% (139 HP)

Cruise speed at 75% power at 6,000 feet (optimum altitude)
full throttle, 2150 RPM ....180 MPH

Standard fuel capacity ....40 gallons

Maximum range (at 165 MPH at 10,000 feet)
with standard tanks ....775 miles, no reserve
with 20-gallon fuselage auxiliary tank
(60 gallons total) ....1180 miles, no reserve

Gross weight ....2725 pounds

Empty weight ....1650 pounds

Useful load ....1075 pounds

Weight available for people and baggage, standard tanks full... 822 pounds

Stall speed (landing, full flaps) ....55 MPH

Rate of climb at sea level ....1100 feet per minute

Service ceiling ....18,000 feet

Airspeed limits Maneuvering ....130 MPH

Maximum structural cruising ....160 MPH

Never exceed ....202 MPH

Flaps extended ....105 MPH

Landing gear extended ....125 MPH

Fuel ....80/87 octane minimum

Essentially a C35 with a few styling and comfort changes, the D35 was the 1953 model and included serials D-3401 through D-3698. Total number built was 298. Gross weight was up 25 pounds and empty weight went up three pounds. Maximum recommended cruise power was increased to 75 percent.

OTHER NEW D35 FEATURES AND CHANGES:

Reclining front seats (adjustable to three positions, 18 degrees of travel).

Optional front seat headrests.

Optional tinted cabin side windows.

Leather interior trim.

36E14 starter.

"Sight and touch" identification of landing gear and flap switches.

The price of the D35 Bonanza was the same as the price of the last 310 C35s . . . $18,990.

E35

BONANZA

Performance with the E-185-11 engine:

Top speed at sea level . . . . .190 MPH
Maximum recommended cruise power . . . . .75% (139 HP)
Cruise speed at 75% power at 6,000 feet (optimum altitude)
    full throttle, 2150 RPM . . . . .180 MPH

Standard fuel capacity . . . . .40 gallons
Maximum range (at 165 MPH at 10,000 feet)
    with standard tanks . . . . .775 miles, no reserve
    with 20-gallon fuselage auxiliary tank
        (60 gallons total) . . . . .1180 miles, no reserve

Gross weight . . . . .2725 pounds
Empty weight . . . . .1675 pounds
Useful load . . . . .1050 pounds
Weight available for people and baggage, standard tanks full. . . 797 pounds

Stall speed (landing, full flaps) . . . . .55 MPH
Rate of climb at sea level . . . . .1100 feet per minute
Service ceiling . . . . .18,000 feet

Performance with the E-225-8 engine:

Top speed at sea level . . . . .194 MPH
Maximum recommended cruise power . . . . .65% (146 HP)
Cruise speed at 65% power at 9,500 feet (optimum altitude)
    full throttle, 2300 RPM . . . . .186 MPH

Standard fuel capacity . . . . .40 gallons
Maximum range (at 165 MPH at 10,000 feet)
    with standard tanks . . . . .775 miles, no reserve
    with 20-gallon fuselage auxiliary tank
      (60 gallons total) . . . . .1180 miles, no reserve

Gross weight . . . . .2725 pounds
Empty weight . . . . .1675 pounds
Useful load . . . . .1050 pounds
Weight available for people and baggage, standard tanks full. . . 797 pounds

Stall speed (landing, full flaps) . . . . .55 MPH
Rate of climb at sea level . . . . .1300 feet per minute
Service ceiling . . . . .19,000 feet

The 225 horsepower model used an 84-inch diameter version of the Beech series 215 propeller. An electric engine primer was also standard with this engine.

Airspeed limits Maneuvering . . . . 130 MPH
                Maximum structural cruising . . . . 175 MPH
                Never exceed . . . . 202 MPH
                Flaps extended . . . . 105 MPH
                Landing gear extended . . . . 125 MPH

Fuel . . . . .80/87 octane minimum

The E35's big feature was its availability with a choice of engines . . . the E-185-11 used in the two preceding models or the new Continental E-225-8 rated at 225 horsepower for takeoff at 2650 RPM (one minute). Manufactured in 1954, serials included D-3699 through D-3998 plus prototype D-3293. Total units produced . . . 301. Empty weight increased 25 pounds over the D35.

OTHER NEW E35 FEATURES AND CHANGES:

Aileron trim control.

Tinted side windows standard.

Two inches more leg room for back seat passengers.

An increase in structural cruising speed to 175 MPH.

THESE CHANGES OCCURRED DURING PRODUCTION:

Aluminum replaced magnesium on the flaps, D-3951 and after.

Flap spotwelds replaced with rivets, D-3951 and after.

Elevator spotwelds replaced with rivets, D-3967 and after.

Revised main wing structure at rear spar (increased strength of rear spar upper cap — standardization with Model 45 Mentor wing) D-3990 and after.

It should be pointed out that with the same horsepower, performance was identical for both versions of the E35 Bonanza.

Price of the E35 Bonanza was $18,990 with the E-185-11; $19,990 with the E-225-8.

$1 million Plane-O-Rama display of new Beechcrafts (1954). The large twin-engine aircraft in the far background is the Beechcraft T-36A designed for the U. S. Air Force. The contract was cancelled just hours before the first flight of the prototype.

F35

BONANZA

Performance with the E-185-11 engine:

Top speed at sea level . . . . .190 MPH
Maximum recommended cruise power . . . . .75% (139 HP)
Cruise speed at 75% power at 6000 feet (optimum altitude)
    full throttle, 2150 RPM . . . . .180 MPH

Standard fuel capacity . . . . .40 gallons
Maximum range (at 165 MPH at 10,000 feet)
    with standard tanks . . . . .775 miles, no reserve
    with 20-gallon wing auxiliary tanks
        (60 gallons total) .1180 miles, no reserve

Gross weight . . . . .2750 pounds
Empty weight . . . . .1697 pounds
Useful load . . . . .1053 pounds
Weight available for people and baggage, standard tanks full. . . 800 pounds

Stall speed (landing, full flaps) . . . . .55 MPH
Rate of climb at sea level . . . . .1100 feet per minute
Service ceiling . . . . .18,000 feet

Performance with the E-225-8 engine:

Top speed at sea level . . . . .194 MPH
Maximum recommended cruise power . . . . .65% (146 HP)
Cruise speed at 65% power at 9,500 feet (optimum altitude)
    full throttle, 2300 RPM . . . . .186 MPH

Standard fuel capacity . . . . .40 gallons
Maximum range (at 165 MPH at 10,000 feet)
    with standard tanks . . . . .775 miles, no reserve
    with 20-gallon wing auxiliary tanks
        (60 gallons total) .1180 miles, no reserve

Gross weight . . . . .2750 pounds
Empty weight . . . . .1697 pounds
Useful load . . . . .1053 pounds
Weight available for people and baggage, standard tanks full. . . 800 pounds

Stall speed (landing, full flaps) . . . . .55 MPH
Rate of climb at sea level . . . . .1300 feet per minute
Service ceiling . . . . .19,000 feet

Airspeed limits Maneuvering . . . . 130 MPH
              Maximum structural cruising . . . . 175 MPH
              Never exceed . . . . 202 MPH
              Flaps extended (normal) . . . . 105 MPH
              Landing gear extended (normal) . . . . 125 MPH

Fuel . . . . .80/87 octane minimum

Like the A35 and C35, the F35 Bonanza was a "big change" model. Power plant options were the same as the E35, but there were many structural, comfort, and utility improvements. The F35 was the 1955 version and included serials D-3999 through D-4391 except D-4376, which was the 1956 G35 Bonanza prototype. Total manufactured . . . 392.

Outwardly, the most noticeable change was the addition of a small, third side window over the baggage compartment on each side of the aircraft. Internally there were many significant changes to accommodate future growth. Structural strength of the wing was increased by extending the spar web and increasing the gauge of the leading edge wing skins. The V-tail was strengthened by increasing the stabilizer spar cap area. Landing gear door attachments were strengthened to permit emergency extension of the landing gear at speeds up to 175 MPH IAS. The F35 was also the first Bonanza to offer (as an option) two ten-gallon auxiliary fuel tanks mounted internally in the wings. These tanks were outboard of the main fuel cells.

Advertised performance of the F35 Bonanza remained the same as that of an E35 Bonanza with the same engine. Empty weight of the F35 went up with its many improvements but allowable gross was increased 25 pounds which resulted in a small net gain in useful load.

OTHER NEW F35 FEATURES AND CHANGES:

Baggage compartment completely upholstered to reduce noise and prevent scuffing of luggage.

Shoulder harnesses in color harmonizing with the upholstery were used.

New larger ashtrays.

New standardized black face instruments.

D-4051 and after had an additional shock cord installed to insure more positive step retraction.

Only a few F35 Bonanzas were manufactured with the E-185-11 engine. The trend to higher power was well established. Price of the F35 was the same as the E35 Bonanza; $18,990 with the E-185-11; $19,990 with the E-225-8.

Bonanza D-4000 and some of the Beechcrafters who built it.

G35

BONANZA

MODEL YEAR 1956

Top speed at sea level . . . . 194 MPH
Maximum recommended cruise power . . . . 75% (169 HP)
Cruise speed at 75% power at 5000 feet (optimum altitude)
     full throttle, 2300 RPM . . . . 190 MPH
Standard fuel capacity . . . . 40 gallons
Maximum range (at 140 MPH at 10,000 feet)
     with standard tanks . . . . 775 miles, no reserve
     with 20-gallon wing auxiliary tanks
         (60 gallons total) . . . . 1170 miles, no reserve
Gross weight . . . . 2775 pounds
Empty weight . . . . 1722 pounds
Useful load . . . . 1053 pounds
Weight available for people and baggage, standard tanks full. . . 800 pounds

Stall speed (landing, full flaps) . . . . 55 MPH
Rate of climb at sea level . . . . 1300 feet per minute
Service ceiling . . . . 19,000 feet

Airspeed limits Maneuvering . . . . 130 MPH
               Maximum structural cruising . . . . 175 MPH
               Never exceed . . . . 202 MPH
               Flaps extended (normal) . . . . 120 MPH
               Landing gear extended (normal) . . . . 140 MPH
Fuel . . . . 80/87 octane minimum

Manufactured in 1956, the G35 Bonanza was the last of the line to use the familiar "E" series Continental engine. It was also the heaviest Bonanza yet . . . empty weight was 164 pounds over that of the original Model 35 . . . but the G35 also represented the apex for that particular power plant/airframe combination. It was even more trouble free than any of its predecessors. Manufacturing and service "squawks" were at a minimum. Serials were D-4392 through D-4865 plus the prototype G35, D-4376, and D-15002. The engine was the E-225-8, but maximum recommended cruise power had been increased to 75 percent. Total manufactured . . . 476.

Except for the higher maximum cruise power, performance of the G35 remained unchanged from the F35 with the exception of weight. Gross weight was up 25 pounds and empty weight also up 25 pounds.

OTHER NEW G35 FEATURES AND CHANGES:

Optional 50 amp generator.

Longer tail pipes for reduced exhaust noise (4⅜-inches longer).

Optional super soundproofing consisting of extra thick blankets of fiber glass and a thicker windshield and windows (¼-inch thick windshield).

Snap-in carpets (quickly removable for cleaning).

Washable, siliconized fabrics.

Clock with time-in-flight feature.

Optional rotating beacon.

Normal gear extension speed increased from 125 MPH to 140 MPH.

Normal flap extension speed increased from 105 MPH to 120 MPH (maximum flap down speed 130 MPH).

Additional wing structural beef-up.

Impact absorbing instrument panel glareshield.

Revised heating system providing a 20 percent increase in cabin heat.

Further improvement in cabin ventilation.

Fully shielded ignition harness for better radio reception.

Improved magneto timing for better engine idling.

Redesigned nose wheel strut for a smoother ride over rough terrain.

Front seat bottom ground adjustable fore and aft.

Improved engine instruments.

Removable rear seat headrests.

Mono-shell tail cone for improved appearance.

Oil separator in engine breather line (to reduce oil on bottom of fuselage) D-4392, D-4425, D-4701 and after.

Over 500 individual improvement changes had been made in the basic Bonanza design by 1956. The G35 was the cumulation of this effort. Price was $21,990. G35 Bonanza D-4758 became the Model 95 Travel Air proto-type, TD-1, then was converted back into Bonanza configuration and designated D-15002. (At this writing this aircraft is owned by John Allen, Plant Manager of Beech's Salina facility.)

N1444G has an unusual history, even for a Bonanza. Originally produced as a G35, it became the Travel Air prototype, then was later converted back to Bonanza configuration and designated D-15002. Heavily modified, it stumps the experts as to its original model identity.

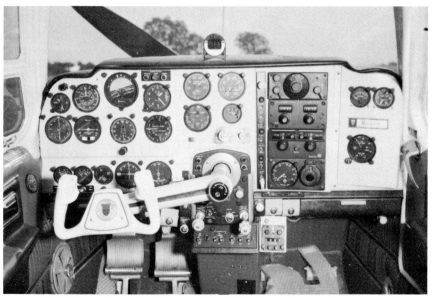

The instrument panel of Bonanza D-15002. Baron type engine gauge and fuel quantity gauges were installed years ahead of their use in production on the 1970 V35B.

91

H35

BONANZA

MODEL YEAR 1957

Top speed at sea level . . . . .206 MPH

Maximum recommended cruise power . . . . .75% (180 HP)

Cruise speed at 75% power at 5000 feet (optimum altitude)
full throttle, 2300 RPM . . . . .196 MPH

Standard fuel capacity . . . . .40 gallons

Maximum range (160 MPH at 10,000 feet)
with standard tanks . . . . .800 miles, no reserve
with 20-gallon wing auxiliary tanks
(60 gallons total) .1170 miles, no reserve

Gross weight . . . . .2900 pounds

Empty weight . . . . .1833 pounds

Useful load . . . . .1067 pounds

Weight available for people and baggage, standard tanks full. . . 810 pounds

Stall speed (landing, full flaps) . . . . .57 MPH

Rate of climb at sea level .1250 feet per minute

Service ceiling . . . . .19,800 feet

Airspeed limits Maneuvering . . . . 142 MPH

Maximum structural cruising . . . . 175 MPH

Never exceed . . . . 210 MPH

Flaps extended (normal) . . . . 120 MPH

Landing gear extended (normal) . . . . 140 MPH

Fuel . . . . .91/96 octane minimum

This model was actually the beginning of a second generation of Bonanzas. It was powered by the first of the "O" series Continental engines, the O-470-G which developed 240 horsepower at 2600 RPM and for the first time, takeoff and maximum continuous horsepower were the same. This engine had many new features in addition to developing more power. It was wet sump, which meant the oil supply was carried internally in the engine and no separate oil tank was required. It also had provisions for a hydraulically controlled and governed propeller. An 84-inch diameter Beech 278-100 propeller was used (first employed on the Beechcraft Mentor). The engine also featured a completely automatic fuel mixture control. The H35 was the only Bonanza to ever have this feature. While earlier Bonanzas were able to use 80 octane fuel, the O-470-G dictated a minimum grade of 91/96 octane for the H35.

Structurally, this Bonanza was considerably different from any of its predecessors. The wing main spar was strengthened by adding more spar cap material and extending the spar web outboard to the wing tip. Actually, the Model 50 Twin-Bonanza spar caps and fittings were used with reduced web gauges. The rear spar was also strengthened. The Twin-Bonanza wing leading edge assembly was used with slight alterations. General structural beef-up also occurred in the nose or keel section, the center section wing carry through structure, and in the fuselage itself in the form of heavier skins and closer rivet spacing in the forward fuselage.

Once again, the tail section came in for its share of changes. The stabilizer assembly was strengthened by the addition of more cap area to the spars, an additional stiffener and rib were added, and the gauge of the spar gusset at the root rib was increased. The elevator was strengthened by the addition of an intermediate inboard and outboard spar. The elevator tab hinge was changed from the formed interlocking design to an extruded hinge section for added strength. Elevator tab area was increased by lengthening the chord two inches. A rib was added. The skin gauge of the tab was also increased. The elevator balance horns were lengthened and increased in gauge to provide proper balance for the added structural weight and the larger trim tab.

The primary flight control system of the H35 remained the same as the earlier Bonanzas, however, the elevator trim tab system was changed increasing the aft bungee spring tension. This resulted in the heavier elevator down spring "feel" which is common on all Bonanzas from the H35 on.

With these structural changes and the new higher powered O-470-G engine, the Bonanza was ready for new, spectacular growth in performance, utility and comfort.

OTHER NEW H35 FEATURES AND CHANGES:

Dynafocal engine mounting.

Electric primer to all six cylinders.

New overhead fresh air system with individual outlets.

50 amp generator standard.

Nylon seat belts with quick adjustment and quick release buckles.

Flush mounted cam-action fuel tank caps with O-ring seals.

Never exceed speed increased from 202 MPH to 210 MPH.

Maneuvering speed increased from 130 MPH to 142 MPH.

Heavier Delco-Remy starter.

Individual front seats (adjustable fore and aft in flight).

Front and rear seat center armrests.

Radio no longer offered as standard equipment.

John Allen, then manager of the Bonanza assembly plant, with an H35, D-5000.

THESE CHANGES OCCURRED DURING PRODUCTION:

Improved engine mounts, D-4866, D-4974, D-5120 and after.

Wire stiffened cold air ducts, D-5141 and after.

Heavier forward belly skin to eliminate canning D-5132 and after.

Additional hole in fuel tank vent lines for added protection from icing, D-5048 and after.

The H35 Bonanza was built during 1957 and encompassed serials D-4866 through D-5330, except for the J35 prototype, D-5062. 464 were manufactured. Price was $22,650.

Many H35s in service today have been retrofitted with Continental's continuous flow fuel injection system.

J35

BONANZA

MODEL YEAR 1958

Top speed at sea level . . . . .210 MPH
Maximum recommended cruise power . . . . .75% (187.5 HP)
Cruise speed at 75% power at 7000 feet (optimum altitude)
     full throttle, 2450 RPM . . . . .200 MPH
Standard fuel capacity . . . . .40 gallons
Maximum range (at 160 MPH at 10,000 feet)
     with standard tanks . . . . .785 miles, no reserve
     with 20-gallon wing auxiliary tanks
          (60 gallons total) .1150 miles, no reserve
Gross weight . . . . .2900 pounds
Empty weight . . . . .1820 pounds
Useful load . . . . .1080 pounds
Weight available for people and baggage, standard tanks full. . . 830 pounds

Stall speed (landing, full flaps) . . . . .57 MPH
Rate of climb at sea level . . . . .1250 feet per minute
Service ceiling . . . . .21,300 feet

Airspeed limits Maneuvering . . . . 142 MPH
               Maximum structural cruising . . . . 185 MPH
               Never exceed . . . . 225 MPH
               Flaps extended (normal) . . . . 120 MPH
               Landing gear extended (normal) . . . . 140 MPH
Fuel . . . . .91/96 octane minimum

The first Bonanza with fuel injection! For that matter, the first postwar business airplane with fuel injection. Basically the J35 was an H35 Bonanza with this one big difference. It was the 1958 model and included serials D-5331 through D-5725 and the J35 prototype, D-5062. Total number produced . . . 396.

The engine was the new Continental IO-470-C which developed 250 horsepower at 2600 RPM. No carburetor (or possibility of carburetor ice) or automatic mixture control, but very precise and even metering of fuel to all cylinders. An extremely smooth and dependable engine, the IO-470-C was the first of a series of Continental fuel injected engines which would power many different airplanes.

Takeoff and maximum continuous horsepower were the same. The propeller was the Beech 278-100 used on the H35 but with an 82-inch diameter.

OTHER NEW J35 FEATURES AND CHANGES:

Electric auxiliary fuel pump (the hand wobble pump was discontinued with this model).

Vernier fuel mixture control.

Instrument panel controls for the firewall fresh air vents (these two vents were previously opened and closed with the foot).

Automatic pilot offered as factory installed optional equipment.

Maximum structural cruising speed increased from 175 MPH to 185 MPH.

Never exceed speed increased from 210 MPH to 225 MPH.

Emergency gear extension speed increased from 175 MPH to 200 MPH.

Large, 3⅛-inch fuel pressure gauge for metering fuel flow more accurately.

Separate fuel quantity gauge for auxiliary tanks.

Louvers installed in engine compartment access doors (to purge lower engine compartment of exhaust heat and avoid fuel vaporization).

Copilot brake pedals removed when dual brakes not installed. This change allowed right hand rudder pedals to be collapsed completely flat when not in use for more leg room.

A horsepower calculator was included in the standard equipment.

The price of the J35 Bonanza was $24,300.

K35

BONANZA

Top speed at sea level . . . . .210 MPH

Maximum recommended cruise power . . . . .75% (187.5 HP)

Cruise speed at 75% power at 7000 feet (optimum altitude)
    full throttle, 2450 RPM . . . . .200 MPH

Standard fuel capacity . . . . .50 gallons

Maximum range (160 MPH at 10,000 feet)
    with standard tanks . . . . .985 miles, no reserve
    with 20-gallon wing auxiliary tanks
        (70 gallons total) .1345 miles, no reserve

Gross weight . . . . .2950 pounds

Empty weight . . . . .1832 pounds

Useful load . . . . .1118 pounds

Weight available for people and baggage, standard tanks full . . . 805 pounds

Stall speed (landing, full flaps) . . . . .59 MPH

Rate of climb at sea level . . . . .1170 feet per minute

Service ceiling . . . . .20,000 feet

Airspeed limits Maneuvering . . . . 142 MPH
                Maximum structural cruising . . . . 185 MPH
                Never exceed . . . . 225 MPH
                Flaps extended (normal) . . . . 120 MPH
                Landing gear extended (normal) . . . . 140 MPH

Fuel . . . . .91/96 octane minimum

98

Manufactured during 1959, the K35 remained substantially unchanged from its predecessor, the J35 Bonanza. Serials D-5726 through D-6161 are K35s. Total manufactured . . . 436.

There was an increase in standard fuel capacity from 40 to 50 gallons. Gross weight was increased 50 pounds over the J35 to accommodate the weight of the additional fuel without substantial penalty to the weight allowance for passengers and baggage.

For the first time an optional fifth seat was offered. Borrowed from the Travel Air, it was side mounted in the baggage area and folded out of the way into a six-inch package when not in use. This was essentially a "jump" seat and not designed to carry a large person. There was also little room for baggage when the seat was occupied. Special "low back" rear seat backs were used when the fifth seat was installed.

With the increase in gross weight, the rate of climb and service ceiling went down slightly and stalling speed increased two MPH.

OTHER NEW K35 FEATURES AND CHANGES:

Individual rear seat backs (adjustable).

Three inches more leg room in the rear seats.

Separate control for the defroster.

Nose gear door extended to completely cover wheel well.

Rudder travel was increased.

The baggage door was strengthened.

Optional dual rotating beacons were offered.

D-5986 and after had tubeless tires.

The price of the K35 was $25,300.

M35

BONANZA

MODEL YEAR 1960

Top speed at sea level . . . . .210 MPH
Maximum recommended cruise power . . . . .75% (187.5 HP)
Cruise speed at 75% power at 7000 feet (optimum altitude)
     full throttle, 2450 RPM . . . . .200 MPH
Standard fuel capacity . . . . .50 gallons
Maximum range (160 MPH at 10,000 feet)
     with standard tanks . . . . .985 miles, no reserve
     with 20-gallon wing auxiliary tanks
          (70 gallons total) .1345 miles, no reserve
Gross weight . . . . .2950 pounds
Empty weight . . . . .1832 pounds
Useful load . . . . .1118 pounds
Weight available for people and baggage, standard tanks full. . . 805 pounds

Stall speed (landing, full flaps) . . . . .59 MPH
Rate of climb at sea level .1170 feet per minute
Service ceiling . . . . .20,000 feet

Airspeed limits Maneuvering . . . . 142 MPH
               Maximum structural cruising . . . . 185 MPH
               Never exceed . . . . 225 MPH
               Flaps extended (normal) . . . . 120 MPH
               Landing gear extended (normal) . . . . 140 MPH
Fuel . . . . .91/96 octane minimum

The 1960 M35 Bonanza was probably the least changed of any of the models. A new high stability wing tip similar in shape to that used on the Beechcraft Super 18 was the one major new feature. Performance was unchanged. Serials were D-6162 through D-6561. Total produced . . . 400.

OTHER NEW M35 FEATURES AND CHANGES:

New matte white instrument markings.

Optional rear seat card table.

The price remained unchanged . . . $25,300.

N35

BONANZA

MODEL YEAR 1961

Top speed at sea level .... 205 MPH

Maximum recommended cruise power .... 75% (195 HP)

Cruise speed at 75% power at 7000 feet (optimum altitude)
full throttle, 2450 RPM .... 195 MPH

Standard fuel capacity .... 50 gallons

Maximum range (at 159 MPH at 10,000 feet)
with standard tanks .... 690 miles
with extended range tanks (80 gallons total) .... 1215 miles

(Ranges include allowance for warm-up, taxi, takeoff, climb, and a 45-minute
reserve at 45% power.)

Gross weight .... 3125 pounds

Empty weight .... 1855 pounds

Useful load .... 1270 pounds

Weight available for people and baggage, standard tanks full... 957 pounds

Stall speed (landing, full flaps) .... 60 MPH

Rate of climb at sea level .... 1150 feet per minute

Service ceiling .... 19,200 feet

Airspeed limits Maneuvering .... 148 MPH
Maximum structural cruising .... 185 MPH
Never exceed .... 225 MPH
Flaps extended (normal) .... 120 MPH
Landing gear extended (normal) .... 140 MPH

Fuel .... 100/130 octane minimum

This was the first of what could be called the "long look" Bonanzas. The 1961 N35 featured a distinctive new rear window which was over twice as big as the window used previously. This change was possible because a utility shelf for light articles had been added which extended 19 inches aft of the rear bulkhead. The N35 also featured a new engine, the Continental IO-470-N which developed 260 horsepower at 2625 RPM. Takeoff and maximum continuous power were the same. Gross weight was increased 175 pounds over the M35 and this resulted in a slight decay in performance. The N35 included serials D-6562 through D-6841. Total produced . . . 280.

OTHER NEW N35 FEATURES AND CHANGES:

Total available internal wing fuel capacity increased from 70 gallons to 80 gallons and the number of fuel tanks reduced from four to two. This was done by offering as an option "extended range capacity" tanks of 40 gallons each in place of the standard tanks of 25 gallons each. Fuel management was now greatly simplified and the possibility of inadvertently taking off or landing while switched to the auxiliary tanks was eliminated.

"Full time" fuel quantity gauges were provided for both tanks. Previous models with four tanks had a left-right switch to monitor fuel capacity separately.

Landing lights were moved to the nose and the nose gear strut. (The new long, leading edge fuel tanks filled the space formerly occupied by the wing landing lights.)

Individual track mounted rear seats with full recline high backs.

Track mounted front seats with full recline feature on right hand seat. (The two right seats could be made into a lounge.) Pilot's seat back was adjustable to four positions.

Flat, safety type control wheel replaced by modern "ram's horn" control wheel.

Bendix 200 magneto system with starting vibrator. (Key operated master switch removed with this change.)

Starter and magneto switches combined into one switch.

Baggage space increased from 16.5 to 22.4 cubic feet with the addition of the new utility shelf.

Shoulder harnesses became optional equipment because of low utilization. (Available for front seats only.)

Optional evaporative type air conditioner discontinued and overhead fresh air system (dry) made standard equipment.

Fixed entrance step (the new utility shelf extended into the area formerly occupied by the step retract mechanism).

Heavy-duty Delco-Remy starter.

Maneuvering speed increased from 142 MPH to 148 MPH.

THESE CHANGES OCCURRED DURING PRODUCTION:

Magnesium on ailerons replaced with aluminum, D-6586 and after.

Scoop for new overhead fresh air system made retractable, D-6686 and after.

One key to operate all locks, D-6786 and after.

The price of the N35 Bonanza was $26,500.

105

P35

BONANZA

Top speed at sea level . . . . .205 MPH

Maximum recommended cruise power . . . . .75% (195 HP)

Cruise speed at 75% power at 7000 feet (optimum altitude)
  full throttle, 2450 RPM . . . . .195 MPH

Standard fuel capacity . . . . .50 gallons

Maximum range (at 159 MPH at 10,000 feet)
  with standard tanks . . . . 690 miles
    with extended range tanks (80 gallons total) . . . . .1215 miles

(Ranges include allowance for warm-up, taxi, takeoff, climb, and a 45-minute
  reserve at 45% power.)

Gross weight . . . . .3125 pounds

Empty weight . . . . .1855 pounds

Useful load . . . . .1270 pounds

Weight available for people and baggage, standard tanks full. . . 948 pounds

Stall speed (landing, full flaps) . . . . .60 MPH

Rate of climb at sea level . . . . .1150 feet per minute

Service ceiling . . . . .19,200 feet

Airspeed limits Maneuvering . . . . 148 MPH

  Maximum structural cruising . . . . 185 MPH

  Never exceed . . . . 225 MPH

  Flaps extended (normal) . . . . 120 MPH

  Landing gear extended (normal) . . . . 165 MPH

Fuel . . . . .100/130 octane minimum

Manufactured during 1962 and 1963, the P35 featured a completely re-designed instrument panel with room for all the electronics anyone could possibly desire. In addition, the radios and the microphone were more centrally located so either front seat occupant could reach them. Flight instruments were grouped in their own separate shock mounted panel in the basic "T" airline type grouping. This panel was hinged for greatly improved access to instruments for servicing.

The familiar "piano keyboard" switch presentation used in all previous Bonanzas was abandoned in favor of a more simplified presentation which included sight and touch identification of the landing gear and flap switches. Circuit breakers were exposed and identified on a lower sub panel.

The P35 series began with serial D-6842 and ran through D-7309 with the exception of D-7140, which was the S35 Bonanza prototype. Total manufactured . . . 467.

Performance remained unchanged from the N35.

OTHER NEW P35 FEATURES AND CHANGES:

Bucket type seats with "omni position" hydrolock reclining mechanisms (pilot's seat back had a four position adjustment).

Optional instrument post lights.

Elevator trim tab indicator repositioned for easier reading.

Extra length rudder pedal arms with needle bearings.

Stall warning horn replaced with a buzzer and stall warning light discontinued.

Normal landing gear extension speed increased to 165 MPH.

Magneto-starter switch, generator and battery switches relocated to left of pilot.

Interior featured high rolled sculptured side-walls.

The spring loaded, low pressure position was eliminated from the auxiliary fuel pump switch.

Installation of flare provisions discontinued because of low utilization.

THESE CHANGES OCCURRED DURING PRODUCTION:

Visual fuel sight tabs added to fuel tank filler necks on D-6975 and after. This enabled linemen to partially fill the tanks with some degree of accuracy.

Post lights added to omni indicator (standard lighting) D-6894 and after.

Improved baggage door sealing, D-7007 and after.

Two-wire fuel gauging system for greater fuel gauge accuracy, D-7080 and after.

6.50 x 8 main wheels and tires replaced by 6.00 x 6 wheels with 7.00 x 6 tires (this change made to utilize new ring disc brakes available with 6.00 x 6 wheels) D-7209 through D-7212, D-7215 and after.

D-7255 and after have an "alternate air" control which can be used to force open the automatic spring loaded alternate air door. This door is located in the side of the intake duct on all Bonanzas and is automatically sucked open if the intake filter is ever clogged with ice or dirt. The control was added to provide the pilot with manual control.

New baggage door latch with separate latching and locking mechanisms, D-7258 and after.

108

P35 Bonanza D-7000 and its proud owner, Beech field, 1962.

Front seats moved inboard three-fourths inch for more shoulder and hip room, D-7083 and after.

Flottorp propeller replaced Beech series 278 propeller, D-7127 and after.

Edgelighted sub-panel placard included with the post light option, D-7047, D-7079 and after.

McCauley propeller replaced Flottorp propeller, D-7239 and after plus D-7216.

The price of the P35 Bonanza was first established at $26,875 and then later increased to $27,650.

S35

BONANZA
MODEL YEARS 1964, 1965

Top speed at sea level . . . . .212 MPH
Maximum recommended cruise power . . . . .75% (214 HP)
Cruise speed at 75% power at 6500 feet (optimum altitude)
    full throttle, 2500 RPM . . . . .205 MPH
Standard fuel capacity . . . . .50 gallons
Maximum range (at 166 MPH at 10,000 feet)
    with standard tanks . . . . 620 miles
    with extended range tanks (80 gallons total) . . . . .1150 miles
(Ranges include allowance for warm-up, taxi, takeoff, climb, and a 45-minute
    reserve at 45% power.)
Gross weight . . . . .3300 pounds
Empty weight . . . . .1885 pounds
Useful load . . . . .1415 pounds
Weight available for people and baggage, standard tanks full. . .1089 pounds
Stall speed (landing, full flaps) . . . . .62 MPH
Rate of climb at sea level . . . . .1200 feet per minute
Service ceiling . . . . .18,300 feet
Airspeed limits Maneuvering . . . . 152 MPH
                Maximum structural cruising . . . . 190 MPH
                Never exceed . . . . 225 MPH
                Flaps extended (normal) . . . . 130 MPH
                Landing gear extended (normal) . . . . 165 MPH
Fuel . . . . .100/130 octane minimum

110

From a purely structural standpoint the S35 Bonanza wasn't a great deal different from the P35, but by every other means of measurement it was the most changed Bonanza to come out of the factory. To begin with, it had new power. Its Continental IO-520-B engine developed 285 horsepower at 2700 RPM. Takeoff and maximum continuous horsepower were the same. The engine had many new features. Nitrided cylinder barrels and crankshaft, sheltered, decongealing oil radiator, oil squirted pistons, and a full flow oil filter, were major improvements. The IO-520-B was also one of the smoothest engines ever to power a Bonanza.

The S35 had a longer cabin. The aft bulkhead was moved back a full 19 inches to provide 11 cubic feet more baggage space for a total of 33.5 cubic feet. Optional forward facing family seats were available for the first time and gave the S35 true big family capability . . . it could carry a family of six in superb comfort.

Speed and load carrying ability were both increased.

OTHER NEW S35 FEATURES AND CHANGES:

Stabi-line power . . . the engine was canted 2½ degrees to the right and 2 degrees down, less rudder power required during takeoff and climb out, and improved longitudinal stability.

A gear-driven alternator capable of developing a full 70 amps of electrical power at only 1700 RPM, 20 amps at idling speeds.

Over-voltage relay to protect electrical equipment from high transient voltages.

Over-voltage light.

Nose gear static ground (automatically grounds airplane on landing) replaced grounding jack points previously installed.

Stall warning buzzer replaced with a horn.

Radio circuits automatically de-energized during starting for protection of transistorized radios.

Longer-life transistorized voltage regulator with reduced radio noise.

Optional, individual forward facing family seats. Seats fold against the aft baggage compartment bulkhead when not in use. (6th seat was available with serial D-7409 and after.)

New cabin heating system providing 30 percent more heat.

Streamlined max-stability wing tips.

Recessed, "no drag" navigation lights.

Two post lights added to sub-panel (standard lighting).

New style, "stinger" tail cone.

Model 33 type pointed elevator balance horns.

Longer, needle nose propeller spinner.

New overhead cabin exhaust vent.

New map storage pockets below the front seats.

New rear window shape (borrowed from the Beechcraft Baron).

Optional three-blade propeller (replaced standard 84-inch two-blade McCauley).

Maneuvering speed increased from 148 MPH to 152 MPH.

Maximum structural cruising speed increased from 185 MPH to 190 MPH.

Flaps extended speed (normal) increased from 120 MPH to 130 MPH.

THESE CHANGES OCCURRED DURING PRODUCTION:

Tubeless tires replaced with tube type tires; main gear, D-7725 and after, nose gear D-7662 and after.

Optional "Magic Hand" automatic landing gear extension system, D-7719, D-7788, and available for D-7842 and after.

Aft cabin air shut-off control, D-7849 and after. This additional control was added to shut off the heat to the two vents behind the front and rear spar carry-through structures. With this control, the pilot can put all available heat in the front of the cabin or on the windshield.

Recessed fuel tank vents (Baron type, to avoid vent icing) D-7829 and after.

Bendix 1200 series magnetos, D-7335 and D-7932 and after.

Optional 5th and 6th seats lowered 1½ inches for more headroom, D-7945 and after.

Dry vacuum pump, D-7920 through D-7926, D-7929 through D-7931.

Optional large 24" x 39" cargo door (replaced the standard 24" x 22" baggage door) D-7416, D-7537, D-7555, and available D-7584 and after.

Bonanza and Baron fuselage mate positions, 1964.

Bonanza and Debonair final assembly line, 1964. Baron line is in background.

All S35 Bonanzas after D-7326 have the supporting structure and floor attachments for the optional 5th and 6th seats even if only standard seating was ordered.

Manufactured during 1964 and 1965 the S35 Bonanza represented a new high in performance, utility, and comfort. D-7140 was the S35 prototype. The series began with serial D-7310 and ended with D-7976 (except D-7859, which became the D33). Total manufactured . . . 667.

The price was $28,750.

V35

BONANZA

V35TC

114

Once again the Bonanza customer had a choice of power plants . . . the normally aspirated Continental 285 horsepower IO-520-B or the turbocharged Continental TSIO-520-D, which also developed 285 horsepower, but was able to hold maximum manifold pressure up to 19,000 feet.

Performance with the normally aspirated IO-520-B (V35):

Top speed at sea level . . . . .210 MPH
Maximum recommended cruise power . . . . .75% (214 HP)
Cruise speed at 75% power at 6500 feet (optimum altitude)
    full throttle, 2500 RPM . . . . .203 MPH

Standard fuel capacity . . . . .50 gallons
Maximum range (at 163 MPH at 10,000 feet)
    with standard tanks . . . . 600 miles
    with extended range tanks (80 gallons total) . . . . .1110 miles
(Ranges include allowance for warm-up, taxi, takeoff, climb, and a 45-minute
    reserve at 45% power.)

Gross weight . . . . .3400 pounds
Empty weight (includes avionics) . . . . .1941 pounds
Useful load . . . . .1459 pounds
Weight available for people and baggage, standard tanks full. . .1127 pounds

Stall speed (landing, full flaps) . . . . .63 MPH
Rate of climb at sea level . . . . .1136 feet per minute
Service ceiling . . . . .17,500 feet

An increase in gross weight to 3400 pounds resulted in a slight reduction in performance when compared with the S35. Empty weight is up because radio is again standard equipment and included.

Performance with the turbocharged TSIO-520-D (V35TC):

Top speed at 19,000 feet . . . . .250 MPH
Maximum recommended cruise power . . . . .75% (214 HP)
Cruise speed at 75% power at 24,000 feet (optimum altitude)
    full throttle, 2500 RPM . . . . .230 MPH

Standard fuel capacity . . . . .50 gallons
Maximum range (at 163 MPH at 10,000 feet)
    with standard tanks . . . . 580 miles
    with extended range tanks (80 gallons total) . . . . .1080 miles
(Ranges include allowance for warm-up, taxi, takeoff, climb, and a 45-minute
    reserve at 45% power.)

Gross weight . . . . .3400 pounds
Empty weight (includes 49 cubic foot oxygen system
    as well as radio) . . . . .2000 pounds
Useful load . . . . .1400 pounds
Weight available for people and baggage, standard tanks full. . .1068 pounds

115

Stall speed (landing, full flaps) . . . . .63 MPH

Rate of climb at sea level . . . . .1225 feet per minute

Service ceiling . . . . .29,500 feet

Airspeed limits Maneuvering . . . . 152 MPH

Maximum structural cruising . . . . 190 MPH

Never exceed . . . . 225 MPH

Flaps extended (normal) . . . . 130 MPH

Landing gear extended (normal) . . . . 165 MPH

Fuel . . . . .100/130 octane minimum

At the same power and altitude, the cruise speeds of the V35 and V35TC were substantially the same. The turbocharged version of the IO-520 had a slightly higher specific fuel consumption which caused the very small reduction in range.

OTHER NEW V35 AND V35TC FEATURES AND CHANGES:

New rear intake fresh air scoop for quieter and more abundant ventilation.

New larger air outlets in cabin overhead.

New one-piece windshield (no center post).

New design cabin heater.

Flap position instrument on instrument panel (replaced flap "up" and "down" lights).

New turn coordinator replaced needle and ball instrument.

Edgelighted audio switch panel with two or more radios.

Miniature audio switches.

Narco Mark 12A radio became standard equipment.

Optional reading lights for 3rd and 4th seats.

Optional Constant Copilot (full time lateral stability augmentation).

THESE CHANGES OCCURRED DURING PRODUCTION:

Positive shut-off valve added to new overhead fresh air system, D-7994 and after.

Control wheel map light option, D-8030 and after as required.

Optional Hartzell 3-blade propeller replaced with new, lightweight McCauley 3-blade, D-8208 and after as required.

Right side oxygen outlets for right seat passengers (with factory installed oxygen system), D-8271 and after as required. Previous installations had all outlets on the left side of cabin.

116

Relay and diode added to external power option to prevent external power of reverse polarity from damaging electrical equipment, D-8296 and after as required.

New style, larger, cast aluminum control wheel, D-8336 and after.

Improved dry vacuum pump, D-8381 and after.

Improved heater ducting (thermoplastic ducts replaced with heavier, stronger fiber glass ducts), D-8390 and after.

Beginning with D-8407 all Turbo Bonanzas and V35s (with oxygen systems) have altitude compensated Scott automatic oxygen flow regulators. Previous installations used a constant flow regulator of 2.5 PSI.

Optional heated propeller de-icing (2-blade), D-8407 and D-8408 and after as required.

Standard Beech antennas TSO'd, D-8460 and after.

New Goodyear multi-disc wheels and brakes, D-8461 and after.

Optional heated propeller de-icing (3-blade), D-8532 and after as required.

Pilot's oxygen mask with microphone included with oxygen system, D-8536 and after as required.

Improved radio cooling (larger blast tube from right hand wing root vent), D-8564 and after.

The V35 and V35TC Bonanzas were the 1966 and 1967 models. Serials began with D-7977 and ran through D-8598. Total produced . . . 622. Price of the V35 was originally $31,425 but was later increased to $32,500. The price of the V35TC was $37,750 and did not change.

The following are the serial numbers of V35TC Bonanzas:

D-8036	D-8190	D-8274	D-8385	D-8496
D-8048	D-8194	D-8279	D-8393	D-8500
D-8057	D-8199	D-8286	D-8400	D-8505
D-8064	D-8205	D-8294	D-8407	D-8509
D-8072	D-8210	D-8300	D-8419	D-8514
D-8075	D-8217	D-8307	D-8427	D-8518
D-8090	D-8225	D-8316	D-8432	D-8526
D-8127	D-8229	D-8323	D-8438	D-8530
D-8133	D-8234	D-8328	D-8447	D-8533
D-8140	D-8239	D-8336	D-8456	D-8540
D-8146	D-8242	D-8346	D-8465	D-8552
D-8153	D-8245	D-8353	D-8470	D-8560
D-8176	D-8249	D-8359	D-8475	D-8567
D-8181	D-8255	D-8366	D-8481	D-8577
D-8184	D-8261	D-8373	D-8485	D-8596
D-8188	D-8267	D-8379	D-8490	

A total of 79 units.

V35A

BONANZA

V35A-TC

118

Performance with the normally aspirated IO-520-B (V35A):

Top speed at sea level . . . . 210 MPH
Maximum recommended cruise power . . . . 75% (214 HP)
Cruise speed at 75% power at 6500 feet (optimum altitude)
    full throttle, 2500 RPM . . . . 203 MPH

Standard fuel capacity . . . . 50 gallons
Maximum range (at 163 MPH at 10,000 feet)
    with standard tanks . . . . 600 miles
    with extended range tanks (80 gallons total) . . . . 1110 miles
(Ranges include allowance for warm-up, taxi, takeoff, climb, and a 45-minute
    reserve at 45% power.)

Gross weight . . . . 3400 pounds
Empty weight (includes standard avionics) . . . . 1958 pounds
Useful load . . . . 1442 pounds

Stall speed (landing, full flaps) . . . . 63 MPH
Rate of climb at sea level . . . . 1136 feet per minute
Service ceiling . . . . 17,500 feet

Performance with the turbocharged TSIO-520-D (V35A-TC):

Top speed at 19,000 feet . . . . 250 MPH
Maximum recommended cruise power . . . . 75% (214 HP)
Cruise speed at 75% power at 24,000 feet (optimum altitude)
    full throttle, 2500 RPM . . . . 230 MPH

Standard fuel capacity . . . . 50 gallons
Maximum range (at 163 MPH at 10,000 feet)
    with standard tanks . . . . 580 miles
    with extended range tanks (80 gallons total) . . . . 1080 miles
(Ranges include allowance for warm-up, taxi, takeoff, climb, and a 45-minute
    reserve at 45% power.)

Gross weight . . . . 3400 pounds
Empty weight (includes 49 cubic foot oxygen system
    as well as standard avionics) . . . . 2021 pounds
Useful load . . . . 1379 pounds

Stall speed (landing, full flaps) . . . . 63 MPH
Rate of climb at sea level . . . . 1225 feet per minute
Service ceiling . . . . 29,500 feet

Airspeed limits Maneuvering . . . . 152 MPH
              Maximum structural cruising . . . . 190 MPH
              Never exceed . . . . 225 MPH
              Flaps extended (normal) . . . . 130 MPH
              Landing gear extended (normal) . . . . 165 MPH

Fuel . . . . 100/130 octane minimum

The 1968 and 1969 versions of the V-tail Bonanzas were called the V35A and V35A-TC. Since 1968 was the year Beech elected to rename the Debonair "Bonanza", it was decided all future V-tail Bonanzas would carry the prefix letter "V" and model changes would be denoted by suffix letters. Hence, V35A, rather than W35.

Although little changed structurally from the V35, the new "A" models did have several worthwhile improvements.

Externally, they could be identified by the new "speed sweep" windshield which borrowed its slope from the Beechcraft Duke. In addition to having 12 degrees more slope than previous windshields, it extended 6 inches farther forward. This allowed more space behind the instrument panel for maintenance.

There was also an unobstructed view forward. The "whip type" ADF sense antenna in front of the windshield (which had served double duty as an ice detector for so long) was discontinued. In its place 10 feet of wire was mounted on the belly of the Bonanza for better reception. The outside air temperature gauge was moved from the windshield to the left cabin wall near the pilot and was lighted for the first time.

The V35A and V35A-TC could also be identified externally by their white landing gear, polished spinners, steerable taxi lights, and of course, a new paint design.

Inside the cabin, there were changes in the interior styling and the instrument panel. Newly manufactured gyros were offered. The gyro horizon was a 3-inch pictorial gyro and the directional gyro was of the new vertical card type. And they were driven by pressure, not vacuum. This meant less contamination, better operation at altitude.

The Brittian B-5P autopilot and Constant Copilot were also pressure operated and took their attitude sensing direct from the turn coordinator, rather than a separate rate gyro behind the instrument panel. When either autopilot was installed, the turn coordinator was powered both electrically and with pressure. This meant that a failure of either power source would not immobilize this instrument.

Instrument lighting was changed from red to the new "blue-white" lighting and the instrument floodlights were moved from the ceiling to the underside of the glareshield. The glareshield style was changed to provide ample overhang for incorporation of these lights and the glareshield itself was improved. It was made of tough polycarbonate to resist warping.

Instrument panels were the usual Beech autumn smoke but with a lower panel trim color to match the interior. Panel paint was a harder, satin finish to resist stains and scratches.

Included in the new interior styling were softer chairs (improved padding) and larger ashtrays. Performance remained unchanged from the V35 and V35-TC. Empty weight increased slightly.

The following are the serial numbers of V35A-TC Bonanzas:

D-8606	D-8705	D-8829	D-8901	D-8992
D-8615	D-8715	D-8835	D-8911	D-9001
D-8625	D-8730	D-8842	D-8921	D-9008
D-8628	D-8744	D-8849	D-8930	D-9019
D-8638	D-8763	D-8855	D-8940	D-9027
D-8652	D-8777	D-8861	D-8951	D-9039
D-8662	D-8790	D-8868	D-8961	D-9048
D-8673	D-8810	D-8875	D-8973	D-9055
D-8681	D-8823	D-8887	D-8982	D-9063
D-8694				

A total of 46 units.

THESE CHANGES OCCURRED DURING PRODUCTION:

Stops added to inboard seat tracks (as well as outboard) to stop deflections in rear seat frame when heavy loads were applied. D-8606 and after except D-8613 through D-8624, D-8626, D-8627, D-8628, D-8630, D-8636, D-8641, D-8645, D-8646, D-8647, D-8650 and D-8651.

Slick magneto model 662 replaced Bendix mags, D-8622, D-8623, D-9000 and after except D-9001, D-9008, D-9019, D-9027, D-9039, D-9048 and D-9055.

Optional electric elevator trim, D-8622, D-8628, D-8841 and after as required.

Inboard armrests (3rd and 4th seats) reinstated, D-8752 and after.

Inside cargo door handle installed (permitted optional cargo door to be used as an exit by 5th and 6th seat passengers) D-8777 and after as required.

Third latch point for cabin door to improve sealing, D-8785 and after.

Copilot seat back adjustment control relocated to left hand side of seat for easier operation, D-8811 and after.

Redesigned seat backs to reduce flexing, D-8844 and after.

Gear down speed increased to 175 MPH. Flaps down speed increased to 140 MPH, D-8872 and after.

Hoskins strobe light available as a factory installed option, D-8862 and after.

Heat and vent ducting redesign, included rear cabin exhaust scoop (aft of windows, left side) also rerouting of heater intake ducts and cold air ducts for better heat distribution in rear of cabin (33 percent improvement), D-8872 and after.

Cargo door inside assist strap, D-8877 and after.

Walter Gunstream (on the right) delivering Bonanza D-9000 to Mr. and Mrs. Lee D. Hagemeister. This was Mr. Hagemeister's fifth Bonanza.

Improved passenger oxygen masks with oxygen system, D-8900 and after as required.

Temperature protection for oil lines on turbocharged engine installation, D-8940 and after.

Standard radio changed from Narco Mark 12A to Narco Mark 16 (solid state), D-8956 and after.

Bullock strobe light replaced Hoskins strobe as optional equipment, D-9007 and after as required.

V35A and V35A-TC serials began with D-8599 and ran through D-9068. Total manufactured . . . 470. The price of the V35A was originally $35,750 but increased at serial D-8872 to $36,850. The V35A-TC started at $40,950 and increased at serial D-8875 to $42,750.

V35B

BONANZA MODEL YEARS: V35B 1970, 1971 V35B-TC 1970

V35B-TC

Performance with the normally aspirated IO-520-B (V35B):

Top speed at sea level . . . . .210 MPH
Maximum recommended cruise power . . . . .75% (214 HP)
Cruise speed at 75% power at 6500 feet (optimum altitude)
    full throttle, 2500 RPM . . . . .203 MPH

Standard fuel capacity . . . . .50 gallons
Maximum range (at 163 MPH at 10,000 feet)
    with standard tanks . . . . .600 miles
    with extended range tanks (80 gallons total) . . . . .1110 miles
(Ranges include allowance for warm-up, taxi, takeoff, climb, and a 45-minute
    reserve at 45% power.)

Gross weight . . . . .3400 pounds
Empty weight (includes standard avionics) . . . . .1972 pounds
Useful load . . . . .1428 pounds

Stall speed (landing, full flaps) . . . . .63 MPH
Rate of climb at sea level . . . . .1136 feet per minute
Service ceiling . . . . .17,500 feet

Performance with the turbocharged TSIO-520-D (V35B-TC):

Top speed at 19,000 feet . . . . .250 MPH
Maximum recommended cruise power . . . . .75% (214 HP)
Cruise speed at 75% power at 24,000 feet (optimum altitude)
    full throttle, 2500 RPM . . . . .230 MPH

Standard fuel capacity . . . . .50 gallons
Maximum range (at 163 MPH at 10,000 feet)
    with standard tanks . . . . .580 miles
    with extended range tanks (80 gallons total) . . . . .1080 miles
(Ranges include allowance for warm-up, taxi, takeoff, climb, and a 45-minute
    reserve at 45% power.)

Gross weight . . . . .3400 pounds
Empty weight (includes a 49 cubic foot oxygen system
    as well as standard avionics) . . . . .2035 pounds
Useful load . . . . .1365 pounds

Stall speed (landing, full flaps) . . . . .63 MPH
Rate of climb at sea level . . . . .1225 feet per minute
Service ceiling . . . . .29,500 feet

Airspeed limits Maneuvering . . . . .152 MPH
              Maximum structural cruising . . . . .190 MPH
              Never exceed . . . . .225 MPH
              Flaps extended (normal) . . . . .140 MPH
              Landing gear extended (normal) . . . . .175 MPH

Fuel . . . . .100/130 octane minimum

The V35B Bonanza was manufactured during 1970 and 1971, however, its companion turbocharged model, the V35B-TC, was not produced during 1971. Only these seven serials are V35B-TC Bonanzas, all manufactured during the first part of 1970: D-9070, D-9078, D-9088, D-9107, D-9131, D-9154 and D-9180.

The V35B and V35B-TC featured three-light landing gear down indication systems, a redesigned switch panel, new improved engine and fuel quantity instruments (Baron type), and a quick opening cowling. Electroluminescent instrument panel placard lighting was used for the first time for brighter, more uniform night lighting. A new option offered was internally lighted instruments. Performance remained unchanged from the V35A and V35A-TC. With the improvements empty weight increased slightly.

OTHER NEW V35B AND V35B-TC FEATURES AND CHANGES:

Anti-slosh fuel cells (to prevent inadvertent unporting of fuel line during slips, skids, and turning takeoffs with low fuel level in tank).

New, lower glareshield with diffused lighting.

New high back seats with molded shell backs.

Quieter, more attractive pilot's storm window.

Self exciting alternator.

New entry and exit assist handle.

Improved armrests.

Optional door courtesy light.

Optional recessed control wheel map light.

Optional Brittian B-VII autopilot.

Thicker pilot's side window.

Improved parking brake handle.

New interior and exterior styling.

126

THESE CHANGES OCCURRED DURING PRODUCTION:

Higher capacity 232CW pressure pump, D-9061, D-9100, D-9105, D-9115 and after.

Smaller diameter control lock pin, D-9094 and after.

Single center armrests to increase hip room (also seat contour change), D-9130 and after.

Landing gear position indication improvement (relay added to landing gear motor to prevent any early "green" indications from the wheel well switches in advance of the motor completing its cycle), D-9177 and after.

Improved storm window seal, D-9192 and after.

Improved Hartwell cowl latch (sliding channel changed from aluminum to stainless steel), D-9218 and after.

All electric vertical readout engine instruments, D-9222 and after.

Metal placards replaced exterior decals, D-9222 and after.

King KX-170 replaced the Narco Mark 16 as the standard radio, D-9222 and after.

Starter relay circuit breaker changed from 5 amp to 10 amp, D-9223 and after.

Improved glareshield attachment, D-9069 and D-9223 and after.

Cleveland wheels and brakes replaced Goodyear wheels and brakes (main gears), D-9193 and after.

Mechanical nose gear position indicator removed, D-9257 and after. (This indicator became redundant upon change to three-light landing gear down indication system.)

Nose wheel scraper deemed unnecessary and removed, D-9274 and after.

Engine damper pin change (IO-520-B became IO-520-BA), D-9278 and after.

Serials of 1970-1971 V35B production started with D-9069 and ended with D-9286. Total manufactured . . . 218. The price of the V35B was originally $39,250. This price was increased to $41,600 during August, 1970. The price of the V35B-TC began at $45,250 and did not change.

V35B

BONANZA

Top speed at sea level . . . . 210 MPH

Maximum recommended cruise power . . . . 75% (214 HP)

Cruise speed at 75% power at 6500 feet (optimum altitude)
full throttle, 2500 RPM . . . . 203 MPH

Standard fuel capacity . . . . 50 gallons

Maximum range (at 163 MPH at 10,000 feet)
with standard tanks . . . . 600 miles
with extended range tanks (80 gallons total) . . . . 1110 miles

(Ranges include allowance for warm-up, taxi, takeoff, climb, and a 45-minute
reserve at 45% power.)

Gross weight . . . . 3400 pounds

Empty weight (includes standard avionics) . . . . 1985 pounds

Useful load . . . . 1415 pounds

Stall speed (landing, full flaps) . . . . 63 MPH

Rate of climb at sea level . . . . 1136 feet per minute

Service ceiling . . . . 17,500 feet

Airspeed limits Maneuvering . . . . 152 MPH
Maximum structural cruising . . . . 190 MPH
Never exceed . . . . 225 MPH
Flaps extended (normal) . . . . 140 MPH
Landing gear extended (normal) . . . . 175 MPH

Fuel . . . . 100/130 octane minimum

The model designation didn't change from the previous model, but nevertheless, the 1972 edition of the V35B is considered a model change. The interior underwent a major redesign which was so extensive that many structural changes had to be made in the cabin — particularly the roof — to accommodate the all new interior. The 1972 V35B Bonanza features a more durable interior with an improved overhead ventilation system and more head room. Cabin chairs and the instrument panel were also restyled. It can also be distinguished from earlier V35Bs by its new paint design. Empty weight is up slightly over that of the 1971 V35B, otherwise performance is unchanged.

Serials of 1972 V35B production start with D-9287. The price was initially $41,600.

129

The Beechcraft Debonair

Early in 1959 Beech decided to enter the market with a new high performance single engine airplane which would be a companion to the Bonanza. The "Debonair" was thus born. It first flew on September 14, 1959.

The need for the Debonair was created by competition. For many years the Bonanza had reigned supreme — no other airplane could match its performance. If an aircraft owner wanted to fly faster than his Piper Tri-Pacer or Cessna 182 could take him, he had only one choice. While he could be happy with his selection, Piper and Cessna certainly could not.

Then in 1958 Piper introduced its new Comanche — an airplane with a four-cylinder, 180 horsepower Lycoming engine — an airplane that would be priced from $8000 to $10,000 below the selling price of a new model Bonanza. Meanwhile, Cessna was already at work on the retractable gear, high wing Cessna 210 which could get close to Bonanza performance and sell for a lower price. While these new entrees didn't exactly match the Bonanza, they did join its class of performance and provided for the first time an opportunity for owners of Piper and Cessna airplanes to step up in "brand".

In an effort to compete more effectively on a price basis, Beech management elected to place on the market a modified version of the Bonanza — an airplane with a distinctive new personality, more directly comparable to its competition, and available for less money than the Bonanza.

The model number picked was "33" and "Debonair"* was selected as the airplane's name. Webster defines "Debonair" as meaning "of good breed, affable, courteous, gay, and jaunty". Beech, however, went farther back than Webster in explaining the selection. In a press release announcing the new airplane they stated the word actually derived from the French "De Bonne Aire", its origin dating back to medieval France when sportsmen worked hard to develop valuable hunting hawks. In speaking of an exceptional bird, the proud owner would call it "De Bonne Aire", which meant to be of good air.

---

*There were some who thought "Debonair" was not a suitable name for an airplane. It is reliably reported one of the first owners received this response from the tower — "Debonair 836 Romeo, you're cleared to land, sweetie". Doubtlessly this owner agreed.

It was decided the Debonair should look as different from the Bonanza as possible and, above all, the famous V-tail should remain a Bonanza exclusive. The Model 33 acquired three tail surfaces — two of which were simply the V-tail laid flat. The third surface, the vertical fin and rudder, was a completely new design.

A 225 horsepower engine was used to hold costs down. The engine was developed by Continental Motors especially for the Debonair. It was six cylinder and utilized many of the features of the other "O" series engines, but had a lower compression ratio and could burn aviation's regular gasoline — 80 octane fuel.

To reduce the cost of the Debonair still further it was necessary to dispense with many of the deluxe features found on the Bonanza. Some features that were retained became optional equipment. Although the airplane was highly competitive and a tremendous value, it did not enjoy any substantial degree of customer acceptance. When compared with the Bonanza, and even some competitive makes, the first Debonairs were almost totally spartan in appearance. To Beech salesmen, long accustomed to Bonanza elegance, it was difficult to get excited over this new Beechcraft.

Beech began a program to dress up the Debonair in 1960. This program continued until in 1967 the Debonair had acquired virtually all the features of a current model Bonanza except the V-tail and longer cabin. A Debonair could even be ordered with the Bonanza's 285 horsepower engine. The price difference naturally narrowed with all these improvements.

The 1968 models of Bonanzas and Debonairs were so similar Beech decided it actually was no longer manufacturing two separate families of high performance, single engine airplanes — but one large family of Bonanzas. From the 1968 models on, all versions of the Model 33 are called "Bonanzas". And, to further complete the transformation, the 1971 F33A acquired the longer Bonanza cabin.

Today the current Model 33 series of Bonanzas enjoys good customer demand. After their initial poor reception the earlier Debonair models have come back strong on the used airplane market and command good prices.

33

DEBONAIR   MODEL YEAR 1960

Top speed at sea level . . . . .195 MPH

Maximum recommended cruise power . . . . .75% (169 HP)

Cruise speed at 75% power at 7000 feet (optimum altitude)
      full throttle, 2450 RPM . . . . .185 MPH

Standard fuel capacity . . . . .50 gallons

Maximum range (at 148 MPH at 10,000 feet)
      with standard tanks . . . . .845 miles, no reserve
      with 20-gallon wing auxiliary tanks
         (70 gallons total) . . . . .1170 miles, no reserve

Gross weight . . . . .2900 pounds

Empty weight . . . . .1730 pounds

Useful load . . . . .1170 pounds

Weight available for people and baggage, standard tanks full. . . 857 pounds

Stall speed (landing, full flaps) . . . . .60 MPH

Rate of climb at sea level . . . . .1010 feet per minute

Service ceiling . . . . .19,800 feet

Airspeed limits Maneuvering . . . . 142 MPH
               Maximum structural cruising . . . . 185 MPH
               Never exceed . . . . 225 MPH
               Flaps extended (normal) . . . . 120 MPH
               Landing gear extended (normal) . . . . 140 MPH

Fuel . . . . .80/87 octane minimum

The first of the Debonairs, the Model 33 was introduced in November, 1959 and continued in production until November of 1960. Serial numbers began with CD-1 and ran through CD-224 plus CD-233, CD-234, CD-236, CD-241 and CD-246 through CD-250. A total of 233 units were manufactured.

The engine was a Continental fuel injected IO-470-J, a six cylinder engine rated at 225 horsepower at 2600 RPM for all operations. The propeller was an 84-inch aluminum alloy Hartzell. It was hydraulically controlled and used a Hartzell governor.

Structurally the Model 33 was very similar to the 1960 M35 Bonanza then being manufactured. Then, as today, the Model 33s and 35s were produced on the same assembly line. They are even licensed under the same FAA Aircraft Specification, No. 3A15, the Model 33 as a 35-33. And, like the Bonanza, the Debonair is licensed in the Utility Category at full gross weight.

The following is a list of the significant differences between an M35 and the first Model 33s in equipment and furnishings.

	1960 M35 BONANZA	1960 MODEL 33 DEBONAIR
Engine	250 HP Continental	225 HP Continental
Minimum octane	91/96	80/87
Tail	V-tail	Conventional
Wheels and tires	6.50 x 8	6.00 x 6
Landing lights	two in wings	one on nose gear
Center windows	openable	not openable
Propeller	Beech	Hartzell
Front seats	track mounted	track mounted
Front seat backs	adjustable	limited ground adjustable
Rear seat backs	separate-adjustable	bench type-fixed
Interior	leather trim	vinyl trim
Wing tips	new high stability	same as 35 thru K35
Engine cooling	cowl flaps	fixed gill
Mixture control	vernier	push-pull
Third window	standard	optional
Step	retractable	fixed
Right hand rudder pedals	standard	optional
Complete exterior paint	standard	optional
Sensitive altimeter	standard	optional
Turn and bank indicator	standard	optional
Rate-of-climb indicator	standard	optional
Clock	standard	optional
Outside air temperature gauge	standard	optional
Cylinder head temperature gauge	standard	optional
Sun visors	standard	optional
Glove box	standard	optional
Oil access door	standard	optional
50 amp generator	standard	optional
Right hand muffler	standard	optional
Aileron trim control	standard	optional
Nose wheel scraper	standard	optional
Tow bar	standard	optional
Firewall fresh air vents	adjustable	non adjustable
Wing navigation light reflectors	standard	not offered
Fresh air ducts thru wing leading edge	2	1
Stall warning	horn and light	light only

THESE CHANGES OCCURRED DURING PRODUCTION:

Provisions for limited ground adjustment to the front seat backs and additional rear seat leg room, CD-47 and after plus CD-1, CD-3, CD-5, CD-35, CD-40 and CD-45.

Increased rudder tab area, CD-108, CD-125 and after.

Redesign of fixed gill for improved cooling, CD-109 and after.

Vertical stabilizer change (added support to trailing edge) CD-114 and after.

Heavier baggage door pan for greater rigidity, CD-22, CD-36, CD-44 and after.

Firewall air vent deflectors added, CD-22 and after.

One 5-inch radio speaker replaced the two smaller speakers previously used, CD-108 and after.

This first model Debonair was almost totally utilitarian in appearance. In an effort to hold the price as close to competition as possible many Bonanza "niceties" were left out of the interior. Consequently the Model 33 was poorly accepted by Beech Dealers who were used to selling only the finest. It also had rough going on the retail market with Piper and Cessna owners who were by now accustomed to a little glitter in their airplanes. The price was only $19,995 for the standard airplane. However, after the initial surge of inventory orders, interest dwindled.

On the used airplane market today these early Debonairs are in demand. The built-in Beechcraft dependability, ruggedness, and performance counts for more here than faded gloss.

A33

DEBONAIR

MODEL YEAR 1961

Top speed at sea level . . . . 195 MPH

Maximum recommended cruise power . . . . 75% (169 HP)

Cruise speed at 75% power at 7000 feet (optimum altitude)
 full throttle, 2450 RPM . . . . 185 MPH

Standard fuel capacity . . . . 50 gallons

Maximum range (at 154 MPH at 10,000 feet)
 with standard tanks . . . . 840 miles, no reserve
 with 20-gallon wing auxiliary tanks
  (70 gallons total) . . . . 1160 miles, no reserve

Gross weight . . . . 3000 pounds

Empty weight . . . . 1745 pounds

Useful load . . . . 1255 pounds

Weight available for people and baggage, standard tanks full . . . 933 pounds

Stall speed (landing, full flaps) . . . . 60 MPH

Rate of climb at sea level . . . . 960 feet per minute

Service ceiling . . . . 18,400 feet

Airspeed limits Maneuvering . . . . 147 MPH
            Maximum structural cruising . . . . 185 MPH
            Never exceed . . . . 225 MPH
            Flaps extended (normal) . . . . 120 MPH
            Landing gear extended (normal) . . . . 140 MPH

Fuel . . . . 80/87 octane minimum

With the 1961 Model A33 a dress-up campaign was begun on the Debonair to increase its salability. Complete exterior paint became standard and more colorful fabrics were offered. Some of the Bonanza trim began to creep back into the airplane.

Serial numbers of the A33 are CD-251 through CD-387 and serials CD-225 through CD-232, CD-235, CD-237 through CD-240, and CD-242 through CD-245. The out-of-sequence serials are Model 33s converted at the factory to Model A33s before delivery. Total manufactured . . . 154.

Gross weight was increased 100 pounds and empty weight went up 15 pounds. Maneuvering speed was increased from 142 MPH to 147 MPH.

OTHER NEW A33 FEATURES AND CHANGES:

A hat shelf was provided.

Complete exterior paint was standard.

These items all became standard equipment: sensitive altimeter, sun visors, glove box, oil access door, aileron trim, nose wheel scraper.

All seats had improved padding.

A front seat center armrest was offered as an option.

An overhead fresh air system was incorporated.

A cabin exhaust air vent was added.

Elevator tab control wheel sensitivity was reduced.

A right hand muffler was added to the super soundproofing option.

THE FOLLOWING CHANGES OCCURRED DURING PRODUCTION:

Dimmer added to landing gear and flap indicator lights, CD-251 and after except CD-386 and CD-387.

A "permmold" oil sump replaced the sand cast sump on CD-301 and after except CD-386 and CD-387. The engine designation then became IO-470-K.

Overhead air scoop made retractable, CD-314 and after except CD-386 and CD-387.

Heavier nose gear (similar to Travel Air, this was a standardization change) CD-371 and after.

A Flottorp propeller replaced the Hartzell on CD-372 and after except CD-386 and CD-387.

The price of the A33 Debonair was $21,750.

B33

DEBONAIR
MODEL YEARS 1962, 1963, 1964

Top speed at sea level .... 195 MPH
Maximum recommended cruise power .... 75% (169 HP)
Cruise speed at 75% power at 7000 feet (optimum altitude)
    full throttle, 2450 RPM .... 185 MPH
Standard fuel capacity .... 50 gallons
Maximum range (at 154 MPH at 10,000 feet)
    with standard tanks .... 650 miles
    with extended range tanks (80 gallons total) .... 1140 miles
(Ranges include an allowance for warm-up, taxi, takeoff, climb and a 45-
    minute reserve at 45% power.)
Gross weight .... 3000 pounds
Empty weight .... 1745 pounds
Useful load .... 1255 pounds
Weight available for people and baggage, standard tanks full... 933 pounds
Stall speed (landing, full flaps) .... 60 MPH
Rate of climb at sea level .... 960 feet per minute
Service ceiling .... 18,400 feet
Airspeed limits Maneuvering .... 147 MPH
               Maximum structural cruising .... 185 MPH
               Never exceed .... 225 MPH
               Flaps extended (normal) .... 120 MPH
               Landing gear extended (normal) .... 165 MPH
Fuel .... 80/87 octane minimum

Manufactured during the latter part of 1961, all of 1962, 1963 and 1964, the B33 Debonair saw a further increase in refinement and enjoyed better customer acceptance. Serials began with CD-388 and continue through CD-813. Total manufactured . . . 426.

The engine was the same used in the A33, the IO-470-K. The changes were in the airframe. The N35 Bonanza leading edge wing fuel tanks were used. This increased total available internal wing capacity to 80 gallons when the larger extended range tanks were ordered. With this change the number of wing tanks reduced from four to two. The B33 also featured the new instrument panel designed for the P35 Bonanza. Aside from a small fillet added to the vertical fin, the only external difference was the new paint design.

Performance was identical to that of the A33 Debonair, except for the increase in range.

OTHER NEW B33 FEATURES AND CHANGES:

Normal landing gear extension speed increased to 165 MPH.

"Full time" fuel quantity gauges were provided for both tanks.

Instrument post lights were offered as an option.

The interior featured high rolled sculptured side walls.

Headrest provisions were provided on all seats and headrests were available as an option.

The stall warning light was replaced with a horn.

Magneto-starter switch, generator and battery switches were relocated to the left of the pilot.

Writing table offered as an option.

Front seat backs adjustable to four positions (in flight).

THESE CHANGES OCCURRED DURING PRODUCTION:

Light over the fuel selector valve, CD-431 and after.

Fuel sight tab added to the fuel tank filler necks, CD-514 and after. (This enabled the tanks to be partially filled with greater accuracy.)

Edgelighted sub-panel placard included with post light option, CD-591 and after.

Front seats moved inboard three-fourths inch for more shoulder and hip room, CD-595 and after.

Two wire fuel gauging system (increased accuracy of fuel quantity gauges) CD-626 and after.

Landing light moved from the nose gear into the nose cowl (this change made to allow use of light for night identification) CD-626 and after.

Thicker baggage door for improved sealing and soundproofing, CD-617 and CD-659 and after.

Alternate air control (for manual operation of automatic spring loaded alternate air door) CD-674 and after.

McCauley propeller replaced the Flottorp propeller, CD-662 and after.

New baggage door latch with separate latching and locking mechanisms, CD-676 and after.

Two post lights added to sub-panel for improved standard night lighting, CD-710 and after.

Stall warning buzzer replaced with a horn, CD-710 and after.

Radio protection relay (removed radios from the electrical system during engine starting for protection of transistors) CD-710 and after.

Two map pockets provided under the front seats, CD-710 and after.

Nose gear static ground (automatically grounded airplane on landing, replaced grounding jack points previously installed) CD-716 and after.

C33 Debonair "ram's horn" control wheel, CD-745, CD-789, CD-803 and after.

The price of the B33 was $21,975 initially and then in April, 1962 it was increased to $22,750 beginning with CD-540. On February 1, 1963 the price was further increased to $23,500 for CD-689 through CD-813.

141

C33

DEBONAIR

Top speed at sea level . . . . 195 MPH
Maximum recommended cruise power . . . . 75% (169 HP)
Cruise speed at 75% power at 7000 feet (optimum altitude)
 full throttle, 2450 RPM . . . . 185 MPH
Standard fuel capacity . . . . .50 gallons
Maximum range (at 154 MPH at 10,000 feet)
 with standard tanks . . . . 650 miles
 with extended range tanks (80 gallons total) . . . . .1170 miles
(Ranges include an allowance for warm-up, taxi, takeoff, climb and a 45-
 minute reserve at 45% power.)
Gross weight . . . . .3050 pounds
Empty weight (includes avionics) . . . . .1826 pounds
Useful load . . . . .1224 pounds
Weight available for people and baggage, standard tanks full. . . 896 pounds
Stall speed (landing, full flaps) . . . . .60 MPH
Rate of climb at sea level . . . . .930 feet per minute
Service ceiling . . . . .17,800 feet
Airspeed limits Maneuvering . . . . 147 MPH
 Maximum structural cruising . . . . 185 MPH
 Never exceed . . . . 225 MPH
 Flaps extended (normal) . . . . 120 MPH
 Landing gear extended (normal) . . . . 165 MPH
Fuel . . . . .80/87 octane minimum

This was the first of the Debonairs to offer the "long look" of the later model Bonanzas. The optional third window was the same size and shape used on the N35 and P35. The C33 also had a full grown dorsal fin which enhanced the exterior appearance and added to the already excellent directional stability. A significant change occurred in the interior where for the first time the rear seats, as well as those in front, were individual track mounted seats with adjustable backs.

Customer response to this model clearly indicated the Debonair had at last found its place in the Beechcraft line. The C33 was produced during 1965, 1966 and 1967. Serials are CD-814 through CD-1118. Total manufactured . . . 305.

Gross weight was increased 50 pounds and this caused a slight decrease in rate of climb and service ceiling when compared with the B33.

OTHER NEW C33 FEATURES AND CHANGES:

Four-color exterior paint design.

New streamlined assist step (Bonanza type).

New "ram's horn" control wheel.

Tubeless tires replaced with tube type tires.

N35 type hat shelf (increased baggage area from 16.5 cubic feet to 22.4 cubic feet).

Additional heater and ventilation duct aft of rear spar.

Larger capacity heater.

Optional factory installed oxygen system.

Right hand wing root fresh air vent added (from the Bonanza).

Wing tip navigation light reflectors added.

Turn and bank, outside air temperature gauge and cylinder head temperature gauge became standard equipment.

THESE CHANGES OCCURRED DURING PRODUCTION:

Optional "Magic Hand" automatic landing gear extension system, CD-826, CD-855, CD-856, CD-895 and after as required.

Softer seats (additional padding), CD-880 and after.

Recessed fuel tank vents (Baron type, to avoid vent icing), CD-888 and after.

Aft cabin air shut-off control, CD-898 and after. This additional control was added to shut off heat to the two vents behind the front and rear spar carry-through structures. The pilot could then put all available heat in the front of the cabin or on the windshield.

Optional emergency static air source, CD-899 and after as required.

An optional 60 amp Ford alternator replaced the optional 50 amp generator, CD-900, CD-910 and after.

Maximum flaps extended speed increased from 120 MPH to 130 MPH, CD-945 and after.

Rear seats raised (comfort improvement), CD-953 and after.

Optional 5th seat (similar to side mounted baggage compartment "jump" seat first introduced on the K35 Bonanza), CD-826 and available on CD-956 and after.

Throttle and propeller controls changed to American Chain and Cable controls (Bonanza) for smoother, more satisfactory operation, CD-964 and after.

Optional "Constant Copilot" (full time lateral stability augmentation) available on CD-976 and after.

Edgelighted audio switch panel (with two or more radios) CD-976 and after.

One-piece windshield (no center post) CD-788, CD-1007 and after.

Turn coordinator replaced turn and bank indicator, CD-1023, CD-1028 and after.

Relocation of fresh air scoop to dorsal fin (quieter, more abundant fresh air), CD-1023, CD-1027 and after.

144

Optional control wheel map light, CD-1008 and after as required.

Flap position indicator gauge (replaced flap "up" and "down" lights), CD-1044 and after.

Heavier stabilizer spar and reinforced aft fuselage to provide common assemblies with the C33A, CD-1051 and after.

Right side oxygen outlets for right seat passengers (with optional factory installed oxygen system), CD-1052 and after as required. Previous installations had all outlets on left side.

Relay and diode added to external power option to prevent external power of reverse polarity from damaging electrical equipment, CD-1057 and after as required.

New style, larger cast aluminum control wheel, CD-1062 and after.

Improved heater ducting (thermoplastic ducts replaced with heavier, stronger fiber glass ducts) CD-1071 and after.

Altitude compensated oxygen regulator included with factory installed oxygen system option, CD-1074 and after as required.

Dry vacuum pump, CD-1073 and after.

Standard Beech antennas TSO'd, CD-1088 and after.

Pilot's oxygen mask with microphone included with factory installed oxygen system option, CD-1105 and after as required.

Goodyear multi-disc wheels and brakes, CD-1106 and after.

Improved radio cooling (larger blast tube from right hand wing root vent), CD-1114 and after.

The price of the C33 Debonair was $23,950 for units CD-814 through CD-896. From CD-897 through CD-1005 the price was $26,425 but this included the Narco Mark 12A with a VOA-4 omni indicator as standard equipment. Beginning with CD-1006 the price was increased to $27,450.

C33A

DEBONAIR

MODEL YEARS 1966, 1967

Top speed at sea level . . . . .208 MPH
Maximum recommended cruise power . . . . .75% (214 HP)
Cruise speed at 75% power at 6500 feet (optimum altitude)
      full throttle, 2500 RPM . . . . .200 MPH
Standard fuel capacity . . . . .50 gallons
Maximum range (at 156 MPH at 10,000 feet)
      with standard tanks . . . . 595 miles
      with extended range tanks (80 gallons total) . . . . .1080 miles
(Ranges include an allowance for warm-up, taxi, takeoff, climb, and a 45-
      minute reserve at 45% power.)
Gross weight . . . . .3300 pounds
Empty weight (includes avionics) . . . . .1888 pounds
Useful load . . . . .1412 pounds
Weight available for people and baggage, standard tanks full. . .1080 pounds
Stall speed (landing, full flaps) . . . . .61 MPH
Rate of climb at sea level . . . . .1200 feet per minute
Service ceiling . . . . .18,300 feet
Airspeed limits Maneuvering . . . . 152 MPH
                 Maximum structural cruising . . . . 190 MPH
                 Never exceed . . . . 225 MPH
                 Flaps extended (normal) . . . . 130 MPH
                 Landing gear extended (normal) . . . . 165 MPH
Fuel . . . . .100/130 octane minimum

146

In February, 1966, Beech began delivering a 285 horsepower version of the C33 Debonair. Designated the C33A, it used the same powerplant as the V35 Bonanza, the Continental IO-520-B. This entry was placed on the market to provide older model Debonair owners a chance to step up in horsepower as well as model and also to compete more effectively with the higher powered Piper Comanches. It was also felt some competitive make owners would trade for a 285 horsepower Debonair who might otherwise be reluctant to move into a V-tail Bonanza or a lower powered 225 horsepower Debonair.

The C33A had its own distinctive paint design to distinguish it from the C33. It was manufactured during 1966 and 1967 and included serials CE-1 through CE-179.

Performance was very close to that of the V35 Bonanza.

The C33A incorporated most of the features of the later production C33 Debonairs. These included:

A one-piece windshield (no center post).

Recessed fuel vents.

Optional 5th seat (side mounted).

Turn coordinator in place of turn and bank instrument.

Optional "Constant Copilot".

Rear seats raised (comfort improvement).

Softer seating.

Aft cabin air shut-off control.

Edgelighted audio switch panel (when two or more radios were ordered).

The C33A also featured the "canted" power plant installation first introduced on the S35 Bonanza. It had these additional features in common with the then current production Bonanzas: cowl flaps, 70 amp gear-driven alternator, vernier mixture control, and needle nose spinner.

147

THESE CHANGES OCCURRED DURING PRODUCTION:

Optional control wheel map light available, CE-2 and after as required.

Relocation of fresh air scoop to the dorsal fin (quieter, more abundant fresh air) with positive shut-off valve, CE-26 and after.

Optional, lightweight McCauley three blade propeller, CE-64 and after as required.

Flap position indicator gauge (replacing flap "up" and "down" lights) CE-60, CE-77 and after.

Right side oxygen outlets for right seat passengers (with optional factory installed oxygen system) CE-91 and after as required. Previous installations had all outlets on left side.

Relay and diode added to external power option to prevent external power of reverse polarity from damaging electrical equipment, CE-102 and after as required.

New style, larger, cast aluminum control wheel, CE-118 and after.

Dry vacuum pump, CE-135 and after.

Improved heater ducting (thermoplastic ducts replaced with heavier, stronger fiber glass ducts) CE-139 and after.

Altitude compensated oxygen regulator included with factory installed oxygen system option, CE-144 and after as required.

C33A Debonair at Aspen, Colorado, December, 1966.

Optional heated propeller de-icing (2-blade), CE-145 and after as required.

Standard Beech antennas TSO'd, CE-151 and after.

Optional heated propeller de-icing (3-blade), CE-163 and after as required.

Pilot's oxygen mask with microphone included with factory installed oxygen system option, CE-165 and after as required.

New Goodyear multi-disc brakes, CE-173 and after.

Improved radio cooling (larger blast tube from right hand wing root vent) CE-173 and after.

Price of the C33A was $29,875 for CE-1 through CE-133. Beginning with CE-134 the price increased to $31,000.

BONANZA

MODEL YEARS 1968, 1969

Top speed at sea level .... 195 MPH
Maximum recommended cruise power .... 75% (169 HP)
Cruise speed at 75% power at 7000 feet (optimum altitude)
    full throttle, 2450 RPM .... 185 MPH
Standard fuel capacity .... 50 gallons
Maximum range (at 142 MPH at 10,000 feet)
    with standard tanks .... 880 miles
    with extended range tanks (80 gallons total) .... 1430 miles
(Ranges include an allowance for warm-up, taxi, takeoff, climb, and a 45-minute reserve at 45% power.)

Gross weight .... 3050 pounds
Empty weight (includes avionics) .... 1862 pounds
Useful load .... 1188 pounds

Stall speed (landing, full flaps) .... 60 MPH
Rate of climb at sea level .... 930 feet per minute
Service ceiling .... 17,800 feet

Airspeed limits Maneuvering .... 147 MPH
               Maximum structural cruising .... 185 MPH
               Never exceed .... 225 MPH
               Flaps extended (normal) .... 130 MPH
               Landing gear extended (normal) .... 165 MPH
Fuel .... 80/87 octane minimum

The Debonair becomes a Bonanza! The Model 33s and 35s had become so similar that with introduction of the E33 model, Beech elected to drop the Debonair name and market a family of Bonanzas.

The E33 was manufactured as a 1968 and 1969 model and was the 225 horsepower version of the "straight tailed" Bonanza. Serials are CD-1119 through CD-1234. Total manufactured . . . 116. With the additional "plush" empty weight, of course, increased over that of the C33. The third window was also made standard for the first time. Range figures will differ from those shown for the C33 Debonair but only because the factory used a slightly different basis for calculation. Performance remained unchanged.

OTHER NEW E33 FEATURES AND CHANGES:

The changes listed briefly here are exactly the same as those shown in more detail in the section on the V35A Bonanza.

New "speed sweep" windshield.

ADF sense antenna moved to the belly of the airplane.

Outside air temperature gauge moved from the windshield to the left cabin wall and lighted.

White landing gear.

Polished spinner.

Optional taxi light made steerable.

New manufacture gyros. Gyro horizon was a 3-inch pictorial gyro and the directional gyro a vertical card type. Gyros were powered by pressure, not vacuum.

The Brittian B-5P autopilot and Constant Copilot were also pressure operated and took their attitude sensing direct from the turn coordinator, rather than a separate rate gyro behind the instrument panel. When either autopilot was installed, the turn coordinator was powered both electrically and with pressure. This meant a failure of either power source would not immobilize this instrument.

New "blue-white" instrument lighting.

Instrument floodlights moved from the ceiling to the underside of the glare-shield.

Improved instrument panel paint and lower panel trim color added.

Improved seat padding.

Larger ashtrays.

New paint design.

THESE CHANGES OCCURRED DURING PRODUCTION:

Stops added to inboard seat tracks (as well as outboard) to stop deflections in rear seat frame when heavy loads were applied. CD-1120, CD-1124 and after except CD-1131 and CD-1132.

Third latch point for cabin door to improve sealing, CD-1171 and after.

Redesigned seat backs to reduce flexing, CD-1189 and after.

Hoskins strobe light available as a factory installed option, CD-1199 and after as required.

Heat and vent ducting redesign including rear cabin exhaust scoop (aft of windows, left side) also rerouting of heater intake ducts and cold air ducts for better heat distribution in rear of cabin (33 percent improvement), CD-1200 and after.

Optional electric elevator trim available, CD-1202 and after as required.

Improved passenger oxygen masks with optional oxygen system, CD-1202 and after as required.

Standard radio changed from Narco Mark 12A to Narco Mark 16 (solid state), CD-1212 and after.

Bullock strobe light replaced Hoskins strobe as optional equipment, CD-1227 and after as required.

Gear down speed increased to 175 MPH. Flap down speed increased to 140 MPH, CD-1200 and after.

The price of the E33 Bonanza was originally set at $30,750. With serial CD-1202 the price was increased to $31,750.

BONANZA

MODEL YEARS 1968, 1969

Top speed at sea level . . . . .208 MPH
Maximum recommended cruise power . . . . .75% (214 HP)
Cruise speed at 75% power at 6500 feet (optimum altitude)
    full throttle, 2500 RPM . . . . .200 MPH
Standard fuel capacity . . . . .50 gallons
Maximum range (at 156 MPH at 10,000 feet)
    with standard tanks . . . . 595 miles
    with extended range tanks (80 gallons total) . . . . .1080 miles
(Ranges include an allowance for warm-up, taxi, takeoff, climb, and a 45-
    minute reserve at 45% power.)
Gross weight . . . . .3300 pounds
Empty weight . . . . .1915 pounds
Useful load . . . . .1385 pounds

Stall speed (landing, full flaps) . . . . .61 MPH
Rate of climb at sea level .1200 feet per minute
Service ceiling . . . . .18,300 feet

Airspeed limits Maneuvering . . . . 152 MPH
                  Maximum structural cruising . . . . 190 MPH
                  Never exceed . . . . 225 MPH
                  Flaps extended (normal) . . . . 130 MPH
                  Landing gear extended (normal) . . . . 165 MPH
Fuel . . . . .100/130 octane minimum

The E33A was simply the 285 horsepower version of the E33, and it was also the first of this model to be called a "Bonanza". Manufactured during 1968 and 1969, the E33A included serials CE-180 through CE-289 except as noted. Total manufactured . . . 79. Performance remained the same as that shown for the C33A with the exception empty weight increased slightly. The third window was made standard beginning with this model.

OTHER NEW E33A FEATURES AND CHANGES:

The changes listed briefly here are exactly the same as those shown in somewhat more detail in the section on the V35A Bonanza.

New "speed sweep" windshield.

ADF sense antenna moved to the belly of the airplane.

Outside air temperature gauge moved from the windshield to the left cabin wall and lighted.

White landing gear.

Polished spinner.

Optional taxi light made steerable.

New manufacture gyros. Gyro horizon was a 3-inch pictorial gyro and the directional gyro a vertical card type. Gyros were powered by pressure, not vacuum.

The Brittian B-5P autopilot and Brittian Constant Copilot were also pressure operated and in addition took their attitude sensing direct from the turn coordinator, rather than a separate rate gyro behind the instrument panel. When either autopilot was installed, the turn coordinator was powered both electrically and with pressure. This meant a failure of either power source would not immobilize this instrument.

New "blue-white" instrument lighting.

Instrument floodlights moved from the ceiling to the underside of the glareshield.

Improved instrument panel paint and lower panel trim color added.

Improved seat padding.

Larger ashtrays.

New paint design.

THESE CHANGES OCCURRED DURING PRODUCTION:

Stops added to inboard seat tracks (as well as outboard) to stop deflections in rear seat frame when heavy loads were applied. CE-182, CE-186, CE-188 and after.

Slick magneto model 662 replaced Bendix mags, CE-181, CE-182, CE-269, CE-276 and after, CJ-25 and after.

Third latch point provided for cabin door to improve sealing, CE-218 and after.

Redesigned seat backs to reduce flexing, CE-234 and after.

Hoskins strobe light available as a factory installed option, CE-237 and after as required.

Gear down speed increased to 175 MPH. Flap down speed increased to 140 MPH, CE-249 and after. Flap speed increased CJ-14 and after.

Optional electric elevator trim available, CE-239 and after as required.

Heat and vent ducting redesign including rear cabin exhaust scoop (aft of windows, left side) also rerouting of heater intake ducts and cold air ducts for better heat distribution in rear of cabin (33 percent improvement), CE-249 and after, CJ-14 and after.

Improved passenger oxygen masks with optional oxygen system, CE-250 and after.

Standard radio changed from Narco Mark 12A to Narco Mark 16 (solid state), CE-261 and after except CE-264 and CE-266, CJ-22 and after.

156

Bullock strobe light replaced Hoskins strobe as optional equipment, CE-276 and after as required, CJ-24 and after as required.

Replaced quick disconnect seat belt end fittings with a fixed type of end fitting, CJ-4, CJ-10, CJ-14 and after.

Fuel reservoir installed in each fuel tank to prevent fuel starvation during slow roll maneuver, CJ-23 and after. (Retrofit kits made available for CJ-1 through CJ-22.)

All references to "CJ" serial designations concern units which were aerobatic versions of the E33A. This model was known as the E33C Aerobatic Bonanza and it is covered on the next page.

These units carried both serial designations but were E33Cs:

CE-236 (CJ-1)	CE-243 (CJ-8)	CE-252 (CJ-15)	CE-261 (CJ-22)
CE-237 (CJ-2)	CE-244 (CJ-9)	CE-253 (CJ-16)	CE-262 (CJ-23)
CE-238 (CJ-3)	CE-245 (CJ-10)	CE-254 (CJ-17)	CE-263 (CJ-24)
CE-239 (CJ-4)	CE-246 (CJ-11)	CE-255 (CJ-18)	CE-269 (CJ-25)
CE-240 (CJ-5)	CE-247 (CJ-12)	CE-257 (CJ-19)	
CE-241 (CJ-6)	CE-248 (CJ-13)	CE-258 (CJ-20)	
CE-242 (CJ-7)	CE-251 (CJ-14)	CE-259 (CJ-21)	

The following serials are from the E33A production block, but they were "Pave Eagle I" airplanes and not standard model E33As:
CE-218, CE-219, CE-221, CE-222, CE-223 and CE-224.

The price of the E33A Bonanza was initially set at $34,150. With serial CE-249 the price was increased to $35,750.

E33B and E33C

BONANZA

MODEL YEARS 1968, 1969

At Utility Category Gross Weight

Top speed at sea level . . . . .208 MPH
Maximum recommended cruise power . . . . .75% (214 HP)
Cruise speed at 75% power at 6500 feet (optimum altitude)
    full throttle, 2500 RPM . . . . .200 MPH

Standard fuel capacity . . . . .50 gallons
Maximum range (at 156 MPH at 10,000 feet)
    with standard tanks . . . . 595 miles
    with extended range tanks (80 gallons total) . . . . .1080 miles
(Ranges include an allowance for warm-up, taxi, takeoff, climb, and a 45-
    minute reserve at 45% power.)

	Utility Category	Acrobatic Category
Gross weight	3300 pounds	2800 pounds
Empty weight (includes standard avionics)	1918 pounds	1918 pounds
Useful load	1382 pounds	882 pounds

At Utility Category Gross Weight

Stall speed (landing, full flaps) . . . . .61 MPH
Rate of climb at sea level . . . . .1200 feet per minute
Service ceiling . . . . .18,300 feet

		Utility Category	Acrobatic Category
Airspeed limits	Maneuvering	152 MPH	165 MPH
	Maximum structural cruising	190 MPH	190 MPH
	Never exceed	225 MPH	234 MPH
	Flaps extended (normal)	130 MPH	130 MPH
	Landing gear extended (normal). .	175 MPH	175 MPH

Fuel . . . . .100/130 octane minimum

During March of 1968 Beech announced that aerobatic versions of the E33 and E33A would be available starting in August of that year. They would be known as the E33B (225 horsepower) and E33C (285 horsepower) and both would be licensed in the FAA Acrobatic Category at 2800 pounds gross weight. Approved maneuvers would be the slow roll, barrel roll, aileron roll, inside loop, Immelman, cuban eight, split-S, single snap roll, vertical reverse, spins, and momentary inverted flight.

Operation in the Acrobatic Category would be limited to the pilot and one passenger. These Bonanzas would be certificated in the Utility Category also and gross weight, CG range, and performance in the Utility Category would be the same as that of the models E33 and E33A.

No E33Bs were sold or manufactured. Customers preferred the higher horse-power of the E33C Bonanza for aerobatics. E33C serials were CJ-1 through CJ-25 for a total of 25 units. Performance in the Utility Category was identical to the E33A. Empty weight increased a few pounds with the additional structure.

CHANGES MADE IN THE BASIC AIRFRAME FOR AEROBATICS INCLUDED:

Aft fuselage — four additional intercostal stringers and an additional bulk-head.
Ailerons — utilized Queen Air Model 65 ribs.
Horizontal stabilizer — had the Travel Air Model 95 type front and rear spars.
Vertical stabilizer — contained heavier leading edge skin and beefed-up spar stubs.
Rudder — decreased rivet spacing.
Rudder cables — larger size.

A comparison of the flight load factors which must be met for the different FAA Categories illustrates the need for additional strength, not just for Acrobatic Category, but for Utility Category as well. Compare the requirements of these two categories with the Normal Category requirements used by most aircraft manufacturers:

	Normal Category	Utility Category	Acrobatic Category
Limit flight load factor (positive)	3.8 G's	4.4 G's	6.0 G's
Ultimate flight load factor (positive)	5.7 G's	6.6 G's	9.0 G's
Limit flight load factor (negative)	1.5 G's	1.8 G's	3.0 G's
Ultimate flight load factor (negative)	2.2 G's	2.7 G's	4.5 G's

160

ADDITIONAL AIRCRAFT EQUIPMENT PROVIDED OVER THAT STANDARD TO THE E33 AND E33A WERE:

A quick release cabin door.

Front seat shoulder harnesses.

G-meter.

Aerobatic fuel boost pump.

Fuel pressure indicator light.

Quickly removable front seat back cushions (to provide additional room for back pack parachutes).

An aerobatic paint design of checkerboard wing tips and tail was also provided.

E33C features were the same as those listed for the E33A. There were, however, several items of optional equipment not approved for use with the aerobatic version. The optional three-bladed propeller was not approved nor were the wing tip fuel tanks. The side mounted 5th seat was not recommended because of the weight involved and the narrow Acrobatic Category CG limits. For a listing of those changes that occurred during production see the section on the E33A.

The price of the E33C was $38,250.

BONANZA

Top speed at sea level .... 195 MPH
Maximum recommended cruise power .... 75% (169 HP)
Cruise speed at 75% power at 7000 feet (optimum altitude)
    full throttle, 2450 RPM .... 185 MPH
Standard fuel capacity .... 50 gallons
Maximum range (at 142 MPH at 10,000 feet)
    with standard tanks .... 880 miles
    with extended range tanks (80 gallons total) .... 1430 miles
(Ranges include an allowance for warm-up, taxi, takeoff, climb, and a 45-minute reserve at 45% power.)
Gross weight .... 3050 pounds
Empty weight (includes standard avionics) .... 1885 pounds
Useful load .... 1165 pounds

Stall speed (landing, full flaps) .... 60 MPH
Rate of climb at sea level .... 930 feet per minute
Service ceiling .... 17,800 feet

Airspeed limits Maneuvering .... 147 MPH
              Maximum structural cruising .... 185 MPH
              Never exceed .... 225 MPH
              Flaps extended (normal) .... 140 MPH
              Landing gear extended (normal) .... 175 MPH
Fuel .... 80/87 octane minimum

A further refinement of the original Model 33. Still using the 225 horse-power Continental IO-470-K, the F33 was the 1970 version and began with serial CD-1235. Like the other 1970 Bonanzas, it featured a 3-light landing gear down indication system, a redesigned switch panel, new improved engine and fuel quantity instruments (Baron type), and a quick opening cowling. Optional internally lighted instruments were available and electroluminescent instrument panel placard lighting was standard for brighter, more uniform night lighting. Performance remained unchanged from the E33. Empty weight increased.

OTHER NEW F33 FEATURES AND CHANGES:

Anti-slosh fuel cells (to prevent inadvertent unporting of fuel line during slips, skids, and turning takeoffs with low fuel level in tank).

Third side window shape changed to that used on the V35B.

New, lower glareshield with diffused lighting.

New high back seats with molded shell backs.

Quieter and more attractive, pilot's storm window.

New entry and exit assist handle.

Improved armrests (optional).

Optional door courtesy light.

Optional recessed control wheel map light.

Optional Brittian B-VII autopilot.

Thicker pilot's side window.

Improved parking brake handle.

New interior and exterior styling.

THESE CHANGES OCCURRED DURING PRODUCTION:

Smaller diameter control lock pin, CD-1240 and after.

Higher capacity 232 CW pressure pump, CD-1244 and after.

Single center armrests (optional) to increase hip room (also seat contour change), CD-1245 and after.

Landing gear position indication improvement (relay added to the landing gear motor to prevent any early "green" indications from the wheel well switches in advance of the motor completing its cycle), CD-1253 and after.

Improved storm window seal, CD-1254 and after.

The F33s are serials CD-1235 through CD-1254. Only 20 units. All were manufactured during 1970 and the price was $34,150.

F33A

BONANZA

Top speed at sea level . . . . .208 MPH

Maximum recommended cruise power . . . . .75% (214 HP)

Cruise speed at 75% power at 6500 feet (optimum altitude)
      full throttle, 2500 RPM . . . . .200 MPH

Standard fuel capacity . . . . .50 gallons

Maximum range (at 156 MPH at 10,000 feet)
      with standard tanks . . . . .595 miles
      with extended range tanks (80 gallons total) . . . . .1080 miles

(Ranges include an allowance for warm-up, taxi, takeoff, climb, and a 45-
      minute reserve at 45% power.)

Gross weight . . . . .3400 pounds

Empty weight (includes standard avionics) . . . . .1933 pounds

Useful load . . . . .1467 pounds

Stall speed (landing, full flaps) . . . . .63 MPH

Rate of climb at sea level . . . . .1136 feet per minute

Service ceiling . . . . .17,500 feet

Airspeed limits Maneuvering . . . . .152 MPH
              Maximum structural cruising . . . . .190 MPH
              Never exceed . . . . .225 MPH
              Flaps extended (normal) .140 MPH
              Landing gear extended (normal) . . . . .175 MPH

Fuel . . . . .100/130 octane minimum

The F33A is one of the more confusing Bonanza models. There were actually two versions, the airplane produced in 1970 and then a "long cabin" version manufactured during 1971.

The 1970 edition was, like its predecessor the E33A, merely a 285 HP model of the current "straight tail" Bonanza. In this case, the F33. Beginning with first deliveries in 1971 the F33A acquired the cabin length of the V35B Bonanza, in other words, an additional 19 inches of aft cabin area. This meant that for the first time a "33" model had the baggage space formerly available in only the "S" and "V" series Model 35s. With this increase in cabin length two of the 35's popular options could also be made available . . . six place family seating and the large cargo door. Beech made the 1971 F33A as much like the V35B as possible by making items previously optional standard to the airplane. These included a leather interior, V35B max-stability wing tips, co-pilot rudder pedals, panel mounted clock, and openable center windows.

Both the 1970 and 1971 F33As featured a three-light landing gear down indication system, a redesigned switch panel, new improved engine and fuel quantity instruments (Baron type), and a quick opening cowling. Optional internally lighted instruments were available and electroluminescent instrument panel placard lighting was standard for brighter, more uniform night lighting. The Aerobatic version was available only in the "short" cabin configuration and only during 1970.

Empty weight increased but so did gross weight, from 3300 pounds to 3400 pounds. With the increase in weight stall speed went up slightly while service ceiling and rate of climb decreased.

165

OTHER NEW F33A FEATURES AND CHANGES:

Anti-slosh fuel cells (to prevent inadvertent unporting of fuel line during slips, skids, and turning takeoffs with low fuel level in the tank).

Third side window shape changed to that used on the V35B.

New, lower glareshield with diffused lighting.

New high back seats with molded shell backs.

Quieter and more attractive pilot's storm window.

New entry and exit assist handle.

Improved center armrests (optional on the 1970 F33A, standard on the 1971 F33A).

Optional door courtesy light.

Optional recessed control wheel map light.

Optional Brittian B-VII autopilot.

Thicker pilot's side window.

Improved parking brake handle.

New interior and exterior styling.

THESE CHANGES OCCURRED DURING PRODUCTION:

Higher capacity 232CW pressure pump, CE-298 and after, CJ-28 and after.

Smaller diameter control lock pin for easier installation, CE-296 and after, CJ-26 and after.

Single center armrests to increase hip room (also seat contour change), CE-300 and after, CJ-29 and after.

Cleveland wheels and brakes replaced Goodyear wheels and brakes, CE-301 and after.

Landing gear position indication improvement (relay added to landing gear motor to prevent any early "green" indications from the wheel well switches in advance of the motor completing its cycle), CE-309 and after, CJ-30 and after.

Improved storm window seal, CE-311 and after.

Improved Hartwell cowl latch (sliding channel changed from aluminum to stainless steel), CE-316 and after except CE-324.

Extended cabin and other V35B features previously listed, CE-316 and after. Empty weight increased to 1965 lbs.

Metal placards replaced exterior decals, CE-312 and after except CE-324.

Starter relay circuit breaker changed from 5 amp to 10 amp, CE-316 and after except CE-324.

Improved glareshield attachment, CE-313 and after except CE-324.

King KX-170 replaced the Narco Mark 16 as the standard radio, CE-316 and after except CE-324.

Mechanical nose gear position indicator removed, CE-339 and after. (This indicator became redundant upon change to the three-light landing gear down indication system.)

Nose wheel scraper deemed unnecessary and removed, CE-349 and after.

Engine damper pin change (IO-520-B became IO-520-BA), CE-346 and after.

Serials of 1970-1971 F33A production started with CE-290 and ended with CE-349. Total manufactured . . . 60 units. The last 34 airplanes had the long cabin. The price of the F33A was initially $38,150. With introduction of the long cabin on CE-316 the price was increased to $41,600, the same as the V35B.

F33C

BONANZA

MODEL YEAR 1970

At Utility Category Gross Weight

Top speed at sea level .... 208 MPH
Maximum recommended cruise power .... 75% (214 HP)
Cruise speed at 75% power at 6500 feet (optimum altitude)
    full throttle, 2500 RPM .... 200 MPH

Standard fuel capacity .... 50 gallons
Maximum range (at 156 MPH at 10,000 feet)
    with standard tanks .... 595 miles
    with extended range tanks (80 gallons total) .... 1080 miles
(Ranges include an allowance for warm-up, taxi, takeoff, climb, and a 45-minute reserve at 45% power.)

	Utility Category	Acrobatic Category
Gross weight	3400 pounds	2800 pounds
Empty weight (includes standard avionics)..	1936 pounds	1936 pounds
Useful load	1464 pounds	864 pounds

At Utility Category Gross Weight

Stall speed (landing, full flaps) .... 63 MPH
Rate of climb at sea level .... 1136 feet per minute
Service ceiling .... 17,500 feet

		Utility Category	Acrobatic Category
Airspeed limits	Maneuvering	152 MPH	165 MPH
	Maximum structural cruising	190 MPH	190 MPH
	Never exceed	225 MPH	234 MPH
	Flaps extended (normal)	140 MPH	140 MPH
	Landing gear extended (normal)..	175 MPH	175 MPH

Fuel ....100/130 octane minimum

Only five 1970 Aerobatic Bonanzas were manufactured . . . CJ-26 through CJ-30. Production of this model was not scheduled for 1971.

F33C features were the same as those listed for the 1970 F33A with the exception none of the F33Cs had anti-slosh fuel cells. The fuel reservoir installed in each tank to prevent fuel starvation during a slow roll (CJ-23 and after) prevented use of the new anti-slosh cells.

All five of these airplanes had new brake fluid reservoirs with check valves to retard leakage during aerobatic maneuvers. Gross weight in the Utility Category increased to 3400 pounds and empty weight went up to 1936 pounds.

For a listing of those changes that occurred during production see the section on the F33A.

The price of the F33C Aerobatic Bonanza was $40,650.

G33

BONANZA

MODEL YEAR 1972

Top speed at sea level . . . . .204 MPH
Maximum recommended cruise power . . . . .75% (195 HP)
Cruise speed at 75% power at 7000 feet (optimum altitude)
    full throttle, 2450 RPM . . . . .193 MPH
Standard fuel capacity . . . . .50 gallons
Maximum range (at 156 MPH at 10,000 feet)
    with standard tanks . . . . .680 miles
    with extended range tanks (80 gallons total) . . . . .1243 miles
(Ranges include an allowance for warm-up, taxi, takeoff, climb, and a 45-
    minute reserve at 45% power.)
Gross weight . . . . .3300 pounds
Empty weight . . . . .1935 pounds
Useful load . . . . .1365 pounds

Stall speed (landing, full flaps) . . . . .57 MPH
Rate of climb at sea level .1060 feet per minute
Service ceiling . . . . .16,600 feet

Airspeed limits Maneuvering . . . . .152 MPH
               Maximum structural cruising . . . . .190 MPH
               Never exceed . . . . .225 MPH
               Flaps extended (normal) .140 MPH
               Landing gear extended (normal) . . . . .175 MPH
Fuel . . . . .100/130 octane minimum

The 1972 G33 was introduced to the Bonanza line to fill the market gap vacated by the F33 during 1970. Biggest single change is additional power. The G33 uses the Continental IO-470-N which develops 260 horsepower maximum continuous at 2625 RPM. This engine was last used on the 1963 P35 Bonanza. Its installation in the G33 differs in this respect, however, it's canted in the same way as the IO-520-B used in the other Bonanzas — two degrees down and two and one-half degrees to the right — less rudder power is required during takeoff and climb out, and there is improvement in longitudinal stability. Another difference is that a 60 amp alternator is used, rather than a 50 amp generator.

The first G33 is CD-1255 which was manufactured in 1971 as the production prototype. This unit has a 1971 interior. All other G33s have the interior improvements common to the rest of the 1972 Bonanza line, more headroom, restyling of interior, chairs, instrument panel, and an improved overhead fresh air system.

The gross weight is 250 pounds higher than the F33 and all other performance is increased.

CD-1256 is the first 1972 G33 and the price is $41,450.

F33A

BONANZA

Top speed at sea level .... 208 MPH
Maximum recommended cruise power .... 75% (214 HP)
Cruise speed at 75% power at 6500 feet (optimum altitude)
     full throttle, 2500 RPM .... 200 MPH
Standard fuel capacity .... 50 gallons
Maximum range (at 156 MPH at 10,000 feet)
     with standard tanks .... 595 miles
     with extended range tanks (80 gallons total) .... 1080 miles
(Ranges include allowance for warm-up, taxi, takeoff, climb, and a 45-minute
     reserve at 45% power.)
Gross weight .... 3400 pounds
Empty weight (includes standard avionics) .... 2000 pounds
Useful load .... 1400 pounds

Stall speed (landing, full flaps) .... 63 MPH
Rate of climb at sea level .... 1136 feet per minute
Service ceiling .... 17,500 feet

Airspeed limits Maneuvering .... 152 MPH
               Maximum structural cruising .... 190 MPH
               Never exceed .... 225 MPH
               Flaps extended (normal) .... 140 MPH
               Landing gear extended (normal) .... 175 MPH
Fuel .... 100/130 octane minimum

No change in model designation from its 1971 counterpart, but the 1972 F33A did experience significant change. The interior underwent a major redesign which was so extensive many structural changes had to be made in the cabin, particularly the roof, to accommodate the all new interior. This model features a more durable interior with more head room and an improved overhead ventilation system. Cabin chairs and the instrument panel were also restyled. Another significant improvement is the change to the all electric vertical readout engine instruments previously introduced on the 1971 V35B. The 1972 F33A has a new paint design to identify it from earlier models. Empty weight is up over that of the 1971 F33A, otherwise performance is unchanged.

Serials of the 1972 F33A production start with CE-350. The price was initially $41,600.

36

BONANZA

MODEL YEARS 1968, 1969

Top speed at sea level ....204 MPH
Maximum recommended cruise power ....75% (214 HP)
Cruise speed at 75% power at 6500 feet (optimum altitude)
    full throttle, 2500 RPM ....195 MPH
Standard fuel capacity ....50 gallons
Maximum range (at 167 MPH at 10,000 feet)
    with standard tanks ....530 miles
    with extended range tanks (80 gallons total) ....980 miles
(Ranges include allowance for warm-up, taxi, takeoff, climb, and a 45-minute
    reserve at 45% power.)
Gross weight ....3600 pounds
Empty weight (includes standard avionics) ....1980 pounds
Useful load ....1620 pounds
Weight available for people and baggage with standard tanks full 1294 pounds
Stall speed (landing, full flaps) ....64 MPH
Rate of climb at sea level ....1015 feet per minute
Service ceiling ....16,000 feet
Airspeed limits Maneuvering ....160 MPH
              Maximum structural cruising ....190 MPH
              Never exceed ....234 MPH
              Flaps extended (normal) ....140 MPH
              Landing gear extended (normal) ....175 MPH
Fuel ....100/130 octane minimum

"The biggest, most versatile Bonanza ever built," that's how Beech described the Bonanza 36. Basically the 36 was an E33A with the aft bulkhead moved back 19 inches (V35A position) and with a 10-inch stretch added in the fuselage. This meant that from bulkhead to bulkhead, the 36 cabin was 29 inches longer than the E33A. It was 10 inches longer than the S35, V35, and V35A Bonanzas and had six cubic feet more cabin area. The stretch was accomplished with only a 31-pound increase in empty weight.

The fuselage (and occupants) actually moved 10 inches farther forward over the wing. This greatly improved the loading envelope and a typically equipped 36 could carry six 170-pound passengers and stay within the center of gravity limits.

It featured a nearly four-foot-wide double door on the right hand side in addition to the customary Bonanza door over the right wing. With the aft doors it was ideal for air ambulance and cargo work. Its cruise speed of 195 MPH made it the fastest six-place, single-engine air taxi available.

Limited accommodations for baggage were provided aft of the 5th and 6th seats and behind the pilot and copilot chairs. This latter arrangement consisted of a baggage web to hold one or more suitcases over the forward spar carry-through structure. The optional 5th and 6th seats could be easily folded up to provide a 40-cubic-foot area for bulky cargo.

The Bonanza 36 had excellent stability throughout its entire CG range. And the 10-inch longer wheel base gave it even better ground balance than that of the other Bonanza models.

Like its contemporaries, the Bonanza 36 was licensed in the Utility Category at its full gross weight of 3600 pounds. The engine was the Continental IO-520-B.

It was offered with a choice of three interiors: deluxe, standard, and utility . . . an interior to fit any job.

OTHER BONANZA 36 FEATURES:

Approved for flight with the rear doors removed.

Door "open" warning light (for rear doors).

New Cleveland ring disc brakes.

Storage compartment in front seat center armrest.

Alternator re-excite feature provided by two, 2-volt dry cells.

Bonded honeycomb construction used in aft doors.

Fin mounted rotating beacon.

(With the exception of the above items, Bonanza 36 features were comparable to those of the other 1968 model Bonanzas.)

THESE CHANGES OCCURRED DURING PRODUCTION:

A third latch point added to the forward cabin door, E-4 and after.

Hoskins strobe light available as an option, E-86 and after as required.

More powerful flap motor, E-106 and after.

Rear cabin exhaust scoop (aft of windows, left side) also rerouting of heater intake ducts and cold air ducts for better heat distribution in rear of cabin (33 percent improvement), E-106 and after.

Optional Hoskins strobe light replaced with lower cost Bullock strobe, E-154 and after as required.

Quickly removable provisions for 5th and 6th seats (quick release pins), E-146 and after.

Prestolite alternator replaced Delcotron alternator, E-124 and after.

Narco Mark 16 replaced Narco Mark 12A as standard radio, E-144 and after.

Slick magnetos replaced Bendix mags, E-156 and after.

The Model 36 Bonanza was introduced June 18, 1968. It was manufactured during the balance of 1968 and during the entire 1969 model year. Serials were E-1 through E-184. The suggested selling price was $40,650.

176

Model 36 Bonanza E-1 in flight with rear doors removed.

Model 36 Bonanzas awaiting mass fly-away from Beech field, June, 1968.

177

BONANZA

MODEL YEARS 1970, 1971

Top speed at sea level . . . . .204 MPH
Maximum recommended cruise power . . . . .75% (214 HP)
Cruise speed at 75% power at 6500 feet (optimum altitude)
    full throttle, 2500 RPM . . . . .195 MPH
Standard fuel capacity . . . . .50 gallons
Maximum range (at 167 MPH at 10,000 feet)
    with standard tanks . . . . .530 miles
    with extended range tanks (80 gallons total) . . . . .980 miles
(Ranges include allowance for warm-up, taxi, takeoff, climb, and a 45-minute
    reserve at 45% power.)
Gross weight . . . . .3600 pounds
Empty weight (includes standard avionics) . . . . .2023 pounds
Useful load . . . . .1577 pounds

Stall speed (landing, full flaps) . . . . .64 MPH
Rate of climb at sea level . . . . .1015 feet per minute
Service ceiling . . . . .16,000 feet

Airspeed limits Maneuvering . . . . .160 MPH
                Maximum structural cruising . . . . .190 MPH
                Never exceed . . . . .234 MPH
                Flaps extended (normal) . . . . .140 MPH
                Landing gear extended (normal) . . . . .175 MPH
Fuel . . . . .100/130 octane minimum

The original Beech factory approach to marketing the Model 36 was to advertise it as an aerial moving van, an air taxi, a carry-all, an ideal charter airplane for the fixed base operator. Although the Model 36 was all of these, this marketing approach didn't sell many airplanes. Most of the firms in the business of charter and air taxi were captive, that is, they were dealers for one of the major airplane manufacturers. Few Piper and Cessna dealers could be swayed into using a Model 36 in their business, and the Beech outlets would use it anyway without this marketing appeal.

Beginning with 1970 production the Model 36 became the A36 and acquired a new look. All the plushness associated with the "V" tail Bonanzas (an interior which had been optional on the first 36s) became standard to the A36. Advertising emphasis was shifted to the owner market which had bought so many Bonanzas over the years.

Features differentiating the A36 from its predecessor are a three-light landing gear down indication system, a redesigned lower instrument panel, new improved engine and fuel quantity instruments (Baron type), and a quick opening cowling. The A36 also features optional internally lighted instruments and standard electroluminescent instrument panel placard lighting for brighter, more uniform night lighting. Empty weight is up over the Model 36, otherwise performance is unchanged.

OTHER NEW A36 FEATURES AND CHANGES:

V35B max-stability wing tips.

New lower glareshield with diffused lighting.

Anti-slosh fuel cells (to prevent inadvertent unporting of fuel line during slips, skids, and turning takeoffs with low fuel in the tank).

New high back seats with molded shell backs.

Quieter and more attractive pilot's storm window.

Thicker pilot's side window.

Self exciting alternator.

Improved armrests.

Optional door courtesy light.

Optional recessed control wheel map light.

Optional Brittian B-VII autopilot.

Improved parking brake handle.

New interior and exterior styling.

THESE CHANGES OCCURRED DURING PRODUCTION:

Smaller diameter control lock pin, E-193 and after.

Higher capacity 232CW pressure pump, E-203 and after.

Single center armrests to increase hip room (also seat contour change), E-209 and after.

Optional club seating available (3rd and 4th seats reversed, facing rearward), E-221 and after as required.

Landing gear position indication improvement (relay added to landing gear motor to prevent any early "green" indications from the wheel well switches in advance of the motor completing its cycle), E-226 and after.

Improved storm window seal, E-232 and after.

Improved Hartwell cowl latch (sliding channel changed from aluminum to stainless steel), E-242 and after.

Metal exterior placards replaced decals, E-243 and after.

Starter relay circuit breaker changed from 5 amp to 10 amp, E-243 and after.

Improved glareshield attachment for easier access to instruments, E-244 and after.

King KX-170 replaced the Narco Mark 16 as the standard radio, E-244 and after.

Mechanical nose gear position indicator removed, E-262 and after. (This indicator system became redundant upon change to the three-light landing gear down indication system.)

Nose wheel scraper deemed unnecessary and removed, E-271 and after.

Engine damper pin change (IO-520-B became IO-520-BA), E-265, E-273 and after.

Serials of 1970-1971 A36 production started with E-185 and ended with E-282. Total manufactured . . . 98 units. The price began at $42,950 but was increased in August, 1970 to $45,550.

BONANZA

Top speed at sea level .... 204 MPH

Maximum recommended cruise power .... 75% (214 HP)

Cruise speed at 75% power at 6500 feet (optimum altitude)
full throttle, 2500 RPM .... 195 MPH

Standard fuel capacity .... 50 gallons

Maximum range (at 167 MPH at 10,000 feet)
with standard tanks .... 530 miles

with extended range tanks (80 gallons total) .... 980 miles

(Ranges include allowance for warm-up, taxi, takeoff, climb, and a 45-minute
reserve at 45% power.)

Gross weight .... 3600 pounds

Empty weight (includes standard avionics) .... 2040 pounds

Useful load .... 1560 pounds

Stall speed (landing, full flaps) .... 64 MPH

Rate of climb at sea level .... 1015 feet per minute

Service ceiling .... 16,000 feet

Airspeed limits Maneuvering .... 160 MPH

Maximum structural cruising .... 190 MPH

Never exceed .... 234 MPH

Flaps extended (normal) .... 140 MPH

Landing gear extended (normal) .... 175 MPH

Fuel .... 100/130 octane minimum

182

Here again no change in model designation, but the 1972 A36 received the same new interior treatment accorded the other 1972 Bonanzas. Cabin chairs and the instrument panel were restyled, and there is additional head room. The overhead ventilation system was also redesigned to bring in more fresh air and to bring it in quieter. Another significant improvement is the change to the all electric vertical readout engine instruments previously introduced on the 1971 V35B. The 1972 A36 has a new paint design to identify it from earlier models. Empty weight is up slightly over that of the 1971 A36, otherwise performance is unchanged.

Serials of the 1972 A36 production start with E-283. The price was initially $45,550.

About Comparison Charts

A comparison chart showing all the Bonanza models side by side has been purposely left out of this book. About all these charts can show is a list of performance numbers. And if you get right down to an apples and apples performance comparison, using the same number of "horses" at the same weights and altitudes, there shouldn't be much difference. A V35 for example, cruising at the maximum recommended cruise power of the Model 35 (115.5 HP) rather than 214 HP, should have about the same cruise speed as the Model 35 if they are both at the same weight and altitude.

To be completely valid, a comparison chart should include all the steps in growth. The many changes and improvements which have allowed the Bonanza to carry more passengers, carry them farther, faster, and in greater comfort and safety. This kind of chart would be difficult to read.

184

Unusual Bonanzas and
Bonanza Modifications

I doubt if anyone has ever attempted to count all the different modifications available for the various Bonanza models, and even if someone did the list would be inaccurate the very next day.

The Beech factory alone has around 50 kits available with which to update and improve the utility of earlier model aircraft and this list changes several times a year. Then there are all the other firms with items ranging from retrofit turbocharging to ski racks. We will make no attempt here to list all these modifications and kits. Some of the companies marketing kits disappear from the scene with unsettling regularity only to reappear, or at least the kit reappears marketed by a different company. Beech Aircraft Corporation and the American Bonanza Society are the best sources for current kit and modification information.

We have included in this section several unusual Bonanzas, some of the more interesting modifications, plus a brief paragraph on additional fuel tanks. The tanks have been made an exception and included because of their utility, particularly for the older models with only two 20-gallon internal wing tanks.

The First "Twin Bonanza", the Model 40

During the latter part of 1948 Beech outfitted a Bonanza with two 180 HP Franklin engines mounted in an "over-under" arrangement in a single nose cowling. They were geared together to drive only one propeller. This, then, was one of the earliest postwar attempts at center-line thrust for a twin.

The design was reportedly abandoned because of the FAA's requirement for a firewall between the two engines. This would have made maintenance on either engine next to impossible.

This photo shows the different upper cowl line necessary plus modified nose gear doors. Because of reduced room the nose gear could not be retracted as far up into the keel section as it is on production Bonanzas.

The Model 40, a Twin Engine Bonanza.

Model 40 power plant. Here you can see the large, complex gear arrangement required to mate two engines to one propeller shaft.

Model 40 power plant installed. The cylinder head cooling fins of the lower
engine are barely visible.

Steve Howbert of Beech (on the left) making delivery of first 35R to Warren Baird. September, 1951.

The Model 35R Bonanza

FAA Aircraft Specification No. A-777 (the type certificate under which Bonanzas Model 35 through G35 are listed) mentions a Model 35R Bonanza. These are remanufactured Model 35s. The factory only converted 13 of the original Bonanzas to 35Rs so these are rare birds indeed.

The program was begun as a customer service during 1951 for owners of the first model Bonanzas. The Korean war was causing delays and shortages in the procurement of materials for new C35 Bonanzas, and production was limited. It was felt this remanufacturing effort would provide a needed alternative. The modifications were extensive, and as a result a Model 35R Bonanza has features and changes found in both the B35 and C35 Bonanzas. The tubular steel center section truss was not replaced as a part of the remanufacture.

Structural changes were made in the wings, tail, and fuselage, and gross weight increased to 2650 pounds. A remanufactured or overhauled E-185-11 was included in the modification, however, takeoff horsepower was limited to 196 HP.

188

OTHER 35R CHANGES:

Model B-200 plastic covered propeller.

Flap travel increased to 30 degrees.

New wobble pump.

New fuel selector valve.

B80 type starter.

Shoulder harnesses for all seats.

New control wheel.

Safe-flight stall warning indicator.

Wing tip light indicators.

Oil access door in cowling.

New improved oil tank.

Battery relocated in firewall.

Access door added to firewall for instrument maintenance.

Cambered elevator tabs.

Wing-root fillets.

Additional air outlet for improved cabin ventilation.

New cabin door lock.

Steerable nose wheel.

Faster actuating landing gear.

Complete new interior and interior soundproofing.

Complete new exterior paint.

The price of the remanufacture varied from $5750 to $6995, depending on the customer's engine and its condition. The work was done at the Beech facility in Herington, Kansas. The remanufacturing effort was not intended as a profit-making venture, but it was soon discovered that at the quoted price it was going to run up sizable losses. With the value of a used 35 at $6000 and the price of a new C35 at $12,990 it was apparent the modification price couldn't be increased.

The project was discontinued in August, 1951, however some of the last 35Rs were delivered in 1952. The aircraft are identified by their original serial number plus a number denoting the order in which they were modified. These are the 35R Bonanzas:

D-25R1	D-588R5	D-1424R8	D-927R11
D-3R2	D-535R6	D-944R9	D-329R12
D-721R3	D-532R7	D-1186R10	D-122R14
D-838R4			

This Super V was manufactured by Bay Aviation Service Company, Oakland, California, in June, 1961. It carried the original Bonanza serial number D-2250 and Super V serial SV-108.

The Super V (Not a Factory Modification)

Designed in 1956 by Mr. David G. Peterson who at the time was chief pilot for Sinclair Oil Company in Tulsa, Oklahoma. The Super V twin-engine modification to the Beechcraft Bonanza has not been a marketing success. Bay Aviation Service Company in San Francisco purchased the design from Peterson and made a few conversions, then in December of 1961 all tooling, engineering data, and the type certificate were sold by Bay to Fleet Aircraft, Inc., of Buffalo, New York. Fleet made an unsuccessful effort to market the modification in 1962 after making several changes to improve serviceability and appearance.

Power was provided by two Lycoming O-360 engines rated at 180 HP. According to Fleet, top speed was 210 MPH, cruise at 55 percent power 184 MPH (optimum altitude), and range 1400 miles at low cruise power. Rate of climb was listed at 1550 FPM, takeoff run 750 feet, and landing roll 600 feet. Minimum single engine control speed . . . 87 MPH. Fuel capacity was 100 gallons. Useful load . . . 1300 pounds.

Like the twin Navion conversions, the Super V was probably condemned from the start by customer reluctance to purchase a reworked single engine airplane. Then too, the availability of the Beechcraft Travel Air and other light twins on the used market destroyed what little potential that might have existed for a modification of this type.

El Dorado Bonanza

The El Dorado Bonanza

Occasionally you may see an older model Bonanza with an "El Dorado" name-plate. This was essentially a kit merchandising program conducted by the Beech factory to improve the utility, appearance, and comfort of earlier model Bonanzas. The El Dorado insignia was earned if a specified group of Beech modification kits were installed on the airplane. Only five kits were actually required.

Kit 35-671-1	complete interior
Kit 35-663-1	"ram's horn" control wheel
Kit 35-646-15	third window (small)
Kit 35-660	extended wing tips (M35 type)
Kit 35-673	El Dorado exterior paint kit

A distinctive El Dorado paint design was recommended to the owner to help identify his Bonanza as something special. The Brittian wing tip fuel tanks, a new overhead console, and the P35 type third window were also available in addition to the five kits required for the "official" nameplate.

The El Dorado program was sold from 1962 through 1965 and then discontinued. The price of the prefabricated interior kits could not be kept competitive with local interior shop charges for the same work. Most of the other modifications are still available as individual kits.

191

The Experimental O35 Bonanza.

The "O" 35 Bonanza

Another one of a kind. The O35 was primarily a 1961 look by the Beech factory at another wing for the Bonanza. It was laminar flow, with multi spar construction which featured an entirely wet leading edge. The major benefits were to be simplicity of construction plus additional internal fuel capacity. There was also a new landing gear which "articulated" upward much the same as the gear on the Beechcraft Musketeer.

This model was never produced for a variety of reasons. Probably most important was the lack of any real gain in performance with the new wing. There were also wing installation and removal problems. From the standpoint of appearance it was thought by some to be a step downward from the production wing and landing gear.

This view shows the laminar flow wing used on the O35 Bonanza. The wet leading edge had fuel tank filler necks at the wing tips. Engine was the Continental 260 horsepower IO-470-N.

D33 "Light Strike" Bonanza.

The Model D33

As of this writing only one has been built, D-7859. This was an S35 Bonanza modified into a special configuration for evaluation of light strike capabilities for the USAF. Tests occurred at Eglin Air Force Base in Florida during July and August of 1965.

Air Force pilots flew this Bonanza with 250-pound napalm bombs, 2.75-inch folding fin unguided rockets, 7.62 mm six-barrel machine guns, bomblet dispensers, 272-pound general purpose bombs, and other ordnance. Six external stores positions were provided for, three under each wing. The two inboard positions were stressed for 600-pound loads and the four outboard positions for 300-pound loads.

The aircraft was also evaluated for such utility uses as parachute drops, forward air control, airborne speaker platform, and leaflet drops. To increase its suitability for these purposes a large rear door was installed in the right side.

Model PD 249 Armed Utility Bonanza.

Model PD249

An improved version of the D33 evaluated at Eglin Air Force Base. The PD 249 is an ordnance delivery aircraft powered by a Continental GIO-520 engine which develops 350 horsepower. The prototype is currently under evaluation.

Pave Eagle I.

Model 1074 "Pave Eagle I"

The first Bonanzas to be used by the U. S. Air Force, Pave Eagle I airplanes were modified E33As powered by basically the same engine used in the Turbo Bonanza. These aircraft have now been removed from active service but they were used for electronic data gathering and could be flown either manned or as a pilotless drone. Additional internal fuel capacity was provided for long missions.

Pave Eagle II (Air Force designation is QU-22B).

Model 1079 "Pave Eagle II"

These are essentially Model 36 Bonanzas, but heavily modified for special data gathering missions. Like their predecessor, they can be flown either as manned aircraft or as pilotless drones. Much information is still classified regarding their performance and mission, but the engine is a high powered turbocharged Continental and the QU-22Bs are capable of a considerable flight endurance.

Flight extender tip tanks installed on an N35 Bonanza.

Wing Tip Fuel Tanks

There are two approved installations, Flight Extenders fifteen-gallon (each) fiber glass tanks and Brittian Industries twenty-gallon (each) metal tanks. The Brittian tanks are marketed by the Beech factory and are approved for all 35 models except the first. They are also approved for most of the Model 33 series.

The Flight Extender tanks are approved for Bonanza Models 35 through S35. Their very early tanks were metal and held twelve gallons each. They later changed to fiber glass construction and increased the capacity to fifteen gallons. A still later version was "canted" much the same as the tip tanks on the Cessna 310. No one is currently producing these tanks.

None of the range data shown in this book includes the use of either of these wing tip tank installations. The increase in range for any particular model can be easily determined by:

— subtracting the standard range from that range shown with fuselage auxiliary tank, internal wing auxiliary tanks, or extended range tanks . . .

— calculating miles per gallon obtained from the additional fuel capacity . . .

— applying this figure to the wing tip tank capacities.

Brittian tip tanks factory installed on a 1971 V35B.

The baggage compartment tank. These tanks were available in capacities of 10 or 20 gallons. Many of the earlier Bonanzas still have this optional tank installed. Some have been removed and replaced with wing tip tanks.

Flying the Bonanza

We are often asked a variety of questions which add up to, *"What is the best way to fly my Bonanza?"*

There is of course no *one* best way, and even if there was it isn't likely we could get unanimous agreement from the vast fraternity of experienced Bonanza pilots — many of them authorities in their own right. This book would not be complete, however, without an attempt to answer some of the most frequently asked questions.

One of the more popular is, *"What manifold pressure and RPM should I use for cruise power?"* The easiest way to handle that one is to suggest the appropriate owner's manual be consulted, but that is side stepping the issue because any number of cruise possibilities are available in the charts. Briefly, my experience has been I seldom have much choice in the power I pull. Here's why. Most Bonanza cross country is at 6500 feet or higher, and at that altitude (unless it's a standard day or colder) I'm running out of 75% power, even with full throttle and maximum recommended cruise RPM. I like to use the maximum recommended cruise power available with the IO-520-B (it's 75%) and at the optimum altitude for that power (for best performance) so I stay around 6500 feet. I believe I would operate any of the "E" series Continentals in the same way — at the maximum recommended cruise power and at the optimum altitude for that power. The only exception would be where the additional range was needed, and that's not often because most of us are ready to land after about three hours of flying anyway.

CRUISE OPERATION

WEIGHT 3400 LBS

NO.	% POWER	ENG SPEED RPM	BHP
1	45	2100	128
2	50	2100	142
3	55	2100	157
4	60	2200	171
5	65	2300	185
6	70	2400	200
7	75	2500	214

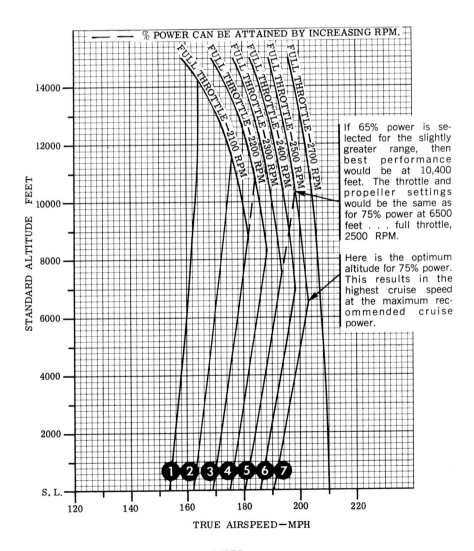

If 65% power is selected for the slightly greater range, then best performance would be at 10,400 feet. The throttle and propeller settings would be the same as for 75% power at 6500 feet . . . full throttle, 2500 RPM.

Here is the optimum altitude for 75% power. This results in the highest cruise speed at the maximum recommended cruise power.

Bonanza V35B

Another frequent question is, *"What should be used for climb power and climb airspeed?"* Again, I vote for the maximum recommended climb power in the owner's manuals, and remember, it will vary with temperature. Many pilots use the same climb manifold pressure, winter or summer, and they are depriving their airplanes of performance on hot days. Then there are others who like to "baby" their engines in climb, and that can lead to trouble. For example, long warm-up periods and/or low power settings in climbs can cause plug fouling in many engines. With regard to climb airspeed, there are three for airplanes in the Bonanza class:

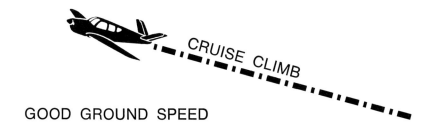

GOOD GROUND SPEED

CRUISE CLIMB — a comfortable rate of ascent with good visibility over the nose. We define cruise climb as a 500 FPM rate of climb at whatever airspeed you are able to indicate at climb power.

MAXIMUM ALTITUDE GAIN

BEST RATE OF CLIMB — maximum altitude gain in a given period of time. Depending on the model, its weight and altitude, best rate of climb airspeed will vary between 100 MPH and 115 MPH. Speed should be reduced approximately 1 MPH for each 1000 feet increase in altitude.

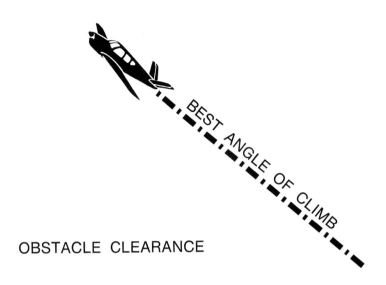

OBSTACLE CLEARANCE

BEST ANGLE OF CLIMB — maximum altitude gain over a given distance. As with best rate of climb, the best angle of climb airspeed will vary with conditions but is usually between 80 MPH and 95 MPH clean. Best angle of climb airspeed increases slightly with altitude.

For ordinary conditions, most Bonanza pilots use cruise climb, it affords good visibility over the nose and is the most comfortable for passengers.

"When should power be reduced after takeoff?" There's no point in being in a hurry. If everything's running fine, why not leave the engine alone until that important first few hundred feet of altitude is obtained?

"What is the best procedure to get the Bonanza 'on the step' in cruise?" We don't believe the Bonanza has this characteristic. In other words, you can either level out at cruise altitude and let the airspeed build up, or you can climb a couple of hundred feet above cruise altitude and build speed rapidly coming back down — the end result will be the same. In the latter instance, you will probably reduce the amount of trimming required.

"What should be used for an approach speed in the Bonanza?" Handbook approach speeds vary between 80 MPH for the 1947 Model 35 up to 90 MPH for the 3600 pound gross Model 36. These speeds should really be labeled "normal over-the-fence speeds". Here's why. The Bonanzas all have the ability to dissipate speed quickly. In jet traffic, and with the later model Bonanzas, you can carry 160 knots almost to the middle marker, cut power, drop the gear, drop flaps, and still make the first turnoff at most jet terminals. Even in the earliest Bonanzas (with lower gear extension speeds) it's possible to use considerably higher than handbook approach numbers when traffic warrants it. All those landing gear doors, struts, braces, and wheels act as very efficient speed brakes. It's a feature not equalled in any other single engine retractable. They are generally "shorter legged" and few have the high gear extension speeds of the late model Bonanzas.

Of course, this feature should be taken into account on a go-around or a 360 degree delaying turn on final approach. The Bonanza is then in a high drag configuration and an entirely different airplane than when it's "clean". Adequate power should be used, and it occasionally takes more than anticipated.

"Should I always use full flaps for landings?" It would be difficult to say always, and this is mostly a matter of choice. However, I know of no factory pilots who use anything but full flaps, even in strong, gusty conditions. If you land the airplane in the same configuration every time you know better how it will react.

"What's the best way to make a short field approach?" The correct speed to use depends a lot on the weight of the aircraft. Short field approach speed for the A36 Bonanza, for example, varies from 62 MPH at 2400 pounds to 80 MPH at 3600 pounds. We have found, in practice, that little is to be gained in trying to reduce these numbers. More important in reducing ground roll is effective use of the brakes, and with the weight distribution of the Bonanza they can be used early and vigorously.

Avoid the low, slow, uncomfortable "drug-in" approach. It's unnecessary in the Bonanza. Gear and flaps should be dropped early and airspeed stabilized, then the appropriate rate of descent established with power. A further decay in airspeed to the recommended minimum can be easily accomplished just seconds before crossing the fence. With the landing gear out and flaps down, the Bonanza can bleed off speed quickly, and there is very little float on landing.

"What about short field takeoffs?" To begin with, there is no benefit in raising the landing gear at the earliest possible moment. The idea is to clear some obstacle, 50 feet or so, and the gear won't be completely retracted until you are well past that altitude. Those inboard landing gear doors moving around could actually cost you some lift.

All of the Bonanza owners' manuals recommend something less than full flaps for short field takeoffs. For the earliest models the manuals state 10 degrees of flap and from the E35 on, 20 degrees. These are conservative settings which provide a short ground run yet a good rate of climb. On rough fields, where the ability to get off the ground quickly because of rocks or high grass is needed, the use of full flaps will appreciably shorten the ground run.

Best angle of climb speed, gear and flaps down, is the same or only slightly above the speed at which the airplane leaves the ground, assuming it is flown off at the earliest possible moment.

"What is the best glide airspeed for maximum distance?" Some early owners' manuals show 100 MPH, the later manuals 122 MPH. The difference is in the gross weight of the aircraft. In other words, at weights lower than gross a new Bonanza's best glide speed for distance would be less than 122 MPH, and this speed would approach the 100 MPH listed for the older models as their weight is approached.

"What is the best way to fly the Bonanza in rough air?" First, let's establish the reason for the question. The Bonanza has a high degree of directional stability, however, it also has the lowest coefficient of drag in its class (Cd .020 in cruise). Because of its compact, low drag profile it has lower damping characteristics than is found in some other airplanes. In rough air the Bonanza will react directionally to gust forces, then, because of its aerodynamic "cleanness" take a little longer to damp out oscillations. Some pilots believe the V-tail is responsible for this characteristic. Actually, it is a very small contributor. The Models 33 and 36, with their conventional tails, share similar characteristics to some degree.

We have found more positive use of the rudder during turns, when raising a wing, etc. will help considerably in rough air. The Bonanza is an excellent "aileron only" airplane in smooth air — in rough air the rudders, or "rudder-vators" become equally important. The Bonanza is not alone in having low damping characteristics — some of today's jet aircraft share the same trait. After about 10 hours most pilots are flying the Bonanza as if they were born in it, and the tendency to let the airplane bounce around in rough air has disappeared.

Flying the Turbo Bonanza

The Continental TSIO-520-D engine was developed from the normally aspi-rated IO-520-B and is identical to it in some respects, but there are impor-tant differences. For example, the compression ratio has been changed from 8.5 to 1 to 7.5 to 1. This is standard practice for new production turbo-charged engines. A lower compression ratio avoids the possibility of detona-tion at the higher induction air temperatures encountered with turbocharging.

Lowering the compression ratio in a normally aspirated engine would result in decreased power. With turbocharging, however, allowable manifold pres-sure is increased to offset this loss. Actually, there are three reasons mani-fold pressures higher than those we are accustomed to using on the IO-520-B should be used on the TSIO-520-D engine:

 — it has a lower compression ratio (to avoid the possibility of deto-nation).

 — it has higher induction air temperatures (from the compression effects of turbocharging) . . . it now takes more air to develop the same power.

 — it has increased exhaust back pressure (a small but measurable loss caused by the turbine in the exhaust system) . . . this is true of all turbocharged systems.

As a result it takes 32.5 inches at 2700 RPM to develop the same 285 horse-power available at 29.6 inches and 2700 RPM on the IO-520-B (sea level, standard day). All climb power and cruise power settings are correspond-ingly higher. This is completely normal for a turbocharged engine, they are designed for it.

EFFECT OF TEMPERATURE ON POWER

Most pilots are aware of the power deterioration of a normally aspirated engine on a hot day. A turbocharged engine experiences an even greater loss at any given manifold pressure — RPM setting. For example, a normally aspirated engine will lose 1% of its power for every 10° F above standard day temperature, even though the same manifold pressure is being used. A turbocharged engine, however, loses 1% for every 6° F above standard, almost twice the loss.

When flying a normally aspirated engine we usually don't give this decay much thought. We are usually at full throttle anyway so there's nothing that can be done about it. With turbocharging, we can often use a higher manifold pressure. Here is an example of 85% climb power settings in the Turbo Bonanza at two extremes in ambient air temperatures:

	10° F	90° F
85% power at 6000 feet pressure altitude	26.4 in., 2500 RPM	29.6 in., 2500 RPM

SYSTEM FEATURES

Many turbocharged aircraft have manifold pressure limits imposed at altitude, limits other than the red line or maximum manifold pressure limit. This is done because of the high induction air temperatures created by high turbine speeds at altitude. Once again, it is to avoid the possibility of detonation. The Turbo Bonanza does not have these restrictions. You can use 32.5 inches of manifold pressure as high as it is available. Under standard day conditions, 32.5 inches is obtainable up to 19,000 feet. On a cold day it can be pulled even higher.

Another big difference in the Bonanza system and others is in the controller. With the "fixed point" controller common to some other systems the turbine is always attempting to supply 32.5 inches of manifold pressure even though the pilot may be asking for much less. The Turbo Bonanza's variable point controller varies the requirement on the turbine with the throttle setting. This means the turbocharger is only working as hard as necessary to produce the induction air needed for that particular power setting. This results in reduced exhaust back pressure and a lower induction air heat rise, and that means greater efficiency.

Also important is the method selected to provide additional cooling air to the engine and turbocharger. In some installations this is accomplished by enlarging the openings in the nose cowl. The Turbo Bonanza has a second set of cowl flaps in the forward engine compartment. By using additional cowl flaps greater cooling is provided, yet the ability is retained to limit air flow for those long descents from altitude. In other words, the Bonanza system provides protection against too rapid cooling, as well as protection from overheating.

Famous Bonanza racing pilot Mrs. Judy Wagner and her K35 Bonanza. Winner of the Powder Puff Derby in 1967, the Angel Derby in 1968, and holder of numerous closed-course pylon racing victories, Judy now flies an Aerobatic Bonanza.

207

Highlights
in Beechcraft Bonanza History

1945:   First flight of Beechcraft Model 35 Bonanza.

1949:   World record for non-stop distance flying for planes of Bonanza category. Capt. Bill Odom in a Beechcraft Bonanza from Honolulu to Oakland, 2406.9 miles in 22 hours, 6 minutes.

1949:   World record for non-stop distance flying for all light planes. Capt. Bill Odom in a Beechcraft Bonanza from Honolulu to Teterboro, N. J., 4957.24 miles in 36 hours, 2 minutes.

1951-
1952:   Around-the-world flight by Congressman Peter F. Mack, Jr., in the same Beechcraft Bonanza Model 35 flown by Bill Odom. Mack covered 30 countries on his solo flight.

1952:   World speed record for light planes, 225.776 km. per hour, set by Paul Burniat of Brussels, Belgium, in a Beechcraft Bonanza.

1953:   Beechcraft Bonanzas finished first, second, third and fourth in first annual Jaycee Transcontinental Air Cruise, Philadelphia to Palm Desert, California. W. H. Hinselman won first place and O. A. Beech Trophy.

1953:   Mrs. Marion Hart, 61-year-old sportswoman, flew non-stop from Newfoundland to Ireland in a Beechcraft Bonanza.

1954:   Mrs. Ann Waddell won O. A. Beech Trophy for fastest speed in annual Skylady Derby, Raton, N. M., to Kansas City, Mo., in a Beechcraft Bonanza.

1954:   Beechcraft Bonanzas finished first, second, and third in the second annual Jaycee Transcontinental Air Cruise from Philadelphia to Palm Desert, Calif. W. C. Butler won first place and O. A. Beech Trophy.

1955:   Mrs. Ann Waddell flew a Beechcraft Bonanza to win the Skylady Derby, Little Rock, Ark., to Raton, N. M.

1956:   Beechcraft Bonanzas win first and second place in the Powder Puff Air Derby. Winning pilot, Mrs. Frances Bera, in a Beechcraft E35 Bonanza.

1957:   Beechcraft Bonanzas win first and third place in the Powder Puff Air Derby. Winning pilot, Mrs. Alice Roberts, in a Beechcraft C35 Bonanza.

1958:   Beechcraft Bonanza wins first place in the Powder Puff Air Derby. Winning pilot, Mrs. Frances Bera, in a Beechcraft A35 Bonanza.

1958:   World record for non-stop distance flying for all light planes. Capt. Pat Boling in a Beechcraft J35 Bonanza from Manila to Pendleton, Oregon, 6856.32 miles, Great Circle distance. (Total miles actually flown — 7090 in 45 hours, 43 minutes.)

1961:   Beechcraft Bonanza wins first place in the Powder Puff Air Derby. Winning pilot, Mrs. Frances Bera, in a Beechcraft E35 Bonanza.

1962:   Beechcraft Bonanza wins first place in the Powder Puff Air Derby. Winning pilot, Mrs. Frances Bera, in a Beechcraft F35 Bonanza.

1967:   Beechcraft Bonanza wins first place in the Powder Puff Air Derby. Winning pilot, Mrs. Judy Wagner, in a Beechcraft K35 Bonanza.

1967:   Beechcraft S35 Bonanza sets three new class speed records while flying around the world. New York to Paris, Tokyo to Point Barrow, Alaska, and Point Barrow to New York. Pilot, Dr. Francis X. Sommer. Copilot, Dr. John Rieger.

1968:   Beechcraft Bonanzas win first and third places in 18th Angel Derby, April 22-25, Managua, Nicaragua, to Panama City, Fla. Mrs. Judy Wagner in Beechcraft K35 Bonanza and Mrs. Pat McEwen in Beechcraft S35 Bonanza.

1969:   Beechcraft S35 Bonanza sets new around-the-world speed record for its class. Thirteen new point-to-point class speed records also set. Pilot, Dr. Hypolite T. Landry.

1969:   Model 36 Bonanza flown by Bill Guinther wins the "Most Meritorious American Entry Prize" in the 1969 London Daily Mail Air Race.

1969:   James W. Gardner and his V35 Bonanza placed first for the third consecutive year as best aircraft in the single engine class at the Reading Air Show.

Classic, 200-mile-an-hour Model 17, the first Beechcraft, set industry standards.

Beechcraft Model 18 prototype was first shown in 1937, to begin 33 consecutive years of production.

Bonanza assembly line, 1966. In the foreground a C33, followed by a C33A and a Turbo Bonanza.

A custom "Sunburst" acrobatic paint design ordered by Atlantic Aviation, Wilmington, Delaware.

C33 Debonair (in background) and C33A Debonair in close formation.

Five of the 20 Beechcraft Debonairs operated by Lufthansa German airlines in their flight training program.

Gear coming up! Inboard main gear doors are completely open for the main wheels.

V35A-TC Bonanza on approach to a short, unimproved strip. The Bonanza landing gear is at home any place.

Bonanza in battle dress, the PD-249.

The 1970 V35B Bonanza in overall white with toreador red stripe and black trim.

215

The Model 36 over man-made Lake Powell in Utah.

The first two Aerobatic Bonanzas, CJ-1 and CJ-2, landing in formation at
Beech field. N775JW is Judy Wagner's airplane.

Beechcraft Beech Aircraft Corporation

Airplane Genealogy Chart

Chronologically tracing the development of business aircraft over 45 years is this genealogy of Beech Aircraft and its predecessor, Travel Air.

Travel Air Company

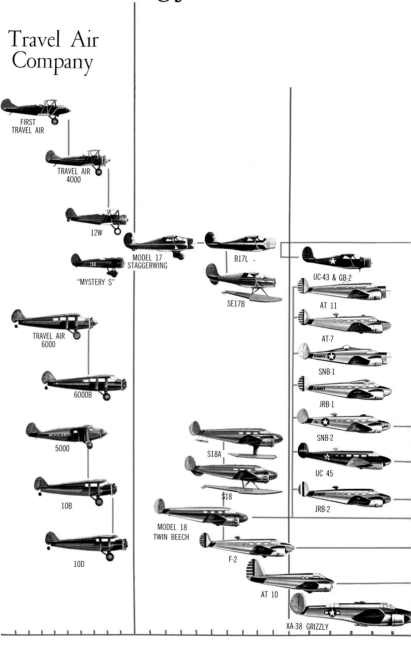

FIRST TRAVEL AIR

TRAVEL AIR 4000

12W

"MYSTERY S"

MODEL 17 STAGGERWING

B17L

SE17B

UC-43 & GB-2

AT 11

AT-7

SNB-1

JRB-1

SNB-2

UC 45

JRB-2

TRAVEL AIR 6000

6000B

5000

10B

10D

S18A

$18

MODEL 18 TWIN BEECH

F-2

AT 10

XA-38 GRIZZLY

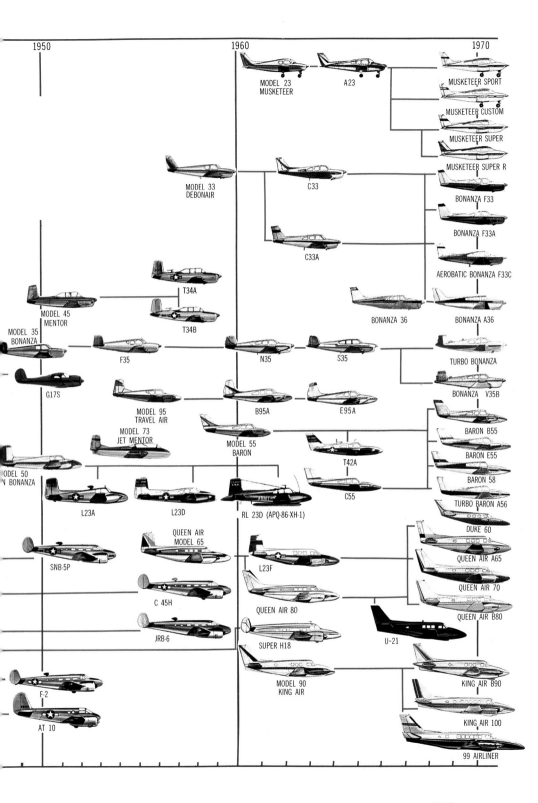

1950   1960   1970

MODEL 23
MUSKETEER

A23

MUSKETEER SPORT

MUSKETEER CUSTOM

MUSKETEER SUPER

MUSKETEER SUPER R

MODEL 33
DEBONAIR

C33

BONANZA F33

C33A

BONANZA F33A

AEROBATIC BONANZA F33C

T34A

MODEL 45
MENTOR

T34B

BONANZA 36

BONANZA A36

MODEL 35
BONANZA

F35

N35

S35

TURBO BONANZA

G17S

BONANZA V35B

MODEL 95
TRAVEL AIR

B95A

E95A

BARON B55

MODEL 73
JET MENTOR

MODEL 55
BARON

T42A

BARON E55

BARON 58

ODEL 50
N BONANZA

L23A

L23D

RL 23D (APQ-86-XH-1)

C55

TURBO BARON A56

DUKE 60

QUEEN AIR
MODEL 65

L23F

QUEEN AIR A65

QUEEN AIR 70

SNB-5P

C 45H

QUEEN AIR 80

U-21

QUEEN AIR B80

JRB-6

SUPER H18

KING AIR B90

F-2

MODEL 90
KING AIR

AT 10

KING AIR 100

99 AIRLINER

219